Turning Points
in Spiritual History

Outline of Esoteric Science
Emil Bock's - The Childhood
of Jesus, The
unknown year

andrew
Welburn - The Book of Fourteen Seals -
pg XXII

Turning Points
in Spiritual History

Six Lectures Held in Berlin
January 19, 1911 – January 25, 1912

Introduction by Edward Reaugh Smith
Edited by Harry Collison
Translated by Walter F. Knox

Rudolf Steiner

SteinerBooks
2007

Originally published in German as *Wendepunkte des Geisteslebens,* Rudolf Steiner-Nachlassverwaltung, Dornach, Switzerland, 1974. The first four lectures also appeared as part of GA 60 and the last two lectures as part of GA 61, Rudolf Steiner Nachlassverwaltung, Dornach, Switzerland. First English edition published by Rudolf Steiner Publishing Co., London, 1934.

SteinerBooks
Anthroposophic Press
610 Main Street, Ste. 1
Great Barrington, Massachusetts 01230
www.steinerbooks.org

Library of Congress Cataloging-in-Publication data is available.

ISBN: 978-0-88010-525-5

Printed in the United States of America

Contents

Introduction

Nothing casual comes to mind when we hear the words *turning point*. Rather we get the idea of a crossroad, a defining or decisive moment, crisis or watershed, a time or incident that marks the beginning of a completely new stage in life or something.

Sometimes the starkness of a situation makes recognition of a turning point immediately obvious. More often the important ones lie concealed until a higher wisdom reveals them in retrospect. For all but the more penetrating vision, history writes the lasting verdict.

We're told in the Bible that the lives of certain notable personalities were predestined from the womb. We should not conclude, however, that the prenatal formation of one's earthly destiny occurs only for the likes of an Isaiah (Is 49,1), Jeremiah (Jer 1,5) or Paul (Gal 1,15) or a Psalmist (Ps 139,16). What existed as predestination in those human beings exists in every human being, as the ancient poet's archetypal human being suggests (Job 14,5).[1]

As we learn from Steiner's works, a series of very significant, periodic turning points is built into our very being. They prescribe our personal destiny, laid into us in the ten classical septennial (seven-year) segments or "septenaries"

---

1. Like the archetypal Cain, Job could not die (Job 1,12; 2,6). That these two were archetypes existing in every human being, see "Cain" and "Job" in Smith, *The Soul's Long Journey*, Great Barrington, SteinerBooks, 2003.

that constitute the seventy years of Psalm 90,10. Recognition of these septenaries is a matter of ancient wisdom.[2] At approximately the beginning of each septenary we come to a natural, cosmically related turning point, predestined during embryonic development through ten moon cycles. Each of the ten classical septenaries relates to one lunar month, or cycle of the moon, during the nine calendar months of the embryonic development in the womb. "The cycle from each new moon to the next one takes 29.5 days, but the actual orbital period of the moon is only 27.3217 days. That is the time it takes the moon to return to (approximately) the same position among the stars" (see *http://www-istp.gsfc.nasa.gov/stargaze/Smoon.htm*). Every human life involves these same *turning points*, always unique to the individual. Most persons willing and able to engage a perceptive intro- and retrospection will be able to recognize them in their own life. The first three, second dentition, puberty and adulthood, at roughly seven-year intervals, are notoriously visible, later ones more subtle though no less meaningful. Just as with those notable biblical personalities, so also is the destiny of each of us formed in our mother's womb

---

2. Philo describes each of them in *De Opificio Mundi* (On the Creation), 103, and in 104 quotes Solon as having recognized and characterized them. In 105 he tells how Hippocrates condenses the ten to seven by combining the fifth through the seventh (ages 28 to 49) and then the last two (ages 56 to 70). Shakespeare also speaks of seven, somewhat similarly arranged, in his *As You Like It*, Act II, Scene VII, lines 139b-161. Steiner speaks of a sevenfold human being in which he combines the fourth through the sixth, with the tenth being of a different nature. So also, it would seem, does the *Corpus Hermiticum*, I, "Poemandres, the Shepherd of Men," 24-26 in tracing the seven planetary stages in the period after earthly life. One's destiny or karmic pattern of life is set in the first nine septenaries, the tenth and beyond being given over to the fruits of that life and preparation for another.

by an unfathomable providence—*turning points* laid into the fabric of our very existence.

It should thus not be hard to imagine that the divine hand that fashions our individual comings and goings also provides something of the same guidance, the same critical *turning points*, in the spiritual life of humanity. In our long human journey, individual and collective, the journey that science calls evolution, many indeed are the turning points. But they are not so much turning points in outer, material manifestation in the fossils of paleontology, for those fossils are only the shed garments worn by humans in an earlier age, vestments designed by providence to meet the need of a changing human consciousness moving through time. Where the real evolution occurs, for which the necessary outer garments are tailored over time, is in the realm of consciousness as it transitions from spirit to matter and back to spirit. Students of Anthroposophy come to know those cosmic influences that come and go as *anthropos* moves from age to age.

It was just such an imagination that caused Marie Steiner, widow of our preeminent seer, soon after his death to select from his massive oeuvre six lectures, each elaborating the immense significance of a personality[3] whose life and work constituted a turning point in the spiritual life of humanity. It should come as no surprise that the last of those chosen is the

---

3. In the exposition of Steiner's works it has become customary to distinguish between a *personality* and an *individuality*. On a soul's long journey through the evolution of humanity, its essential being, its *individuality*, is its Ego or its *I Am*, the part that goes through the cycles of incarnation and excarnation as it works its way toward eventual perfection by taking the higher Christ *I Am* into its being. A *personality* is a partial representation of that individuality as it appears in any single earthly incarnation. *(Continued on following page)*

One great turning point of time, the Christ event, the Mystery of Golgotha for which all others were but preparation.

Nor should her choice of title for the collection, *Turning Points in Spiritual History,* be tampered with, for it would be hard to improve upon.

That all the selected personalities were biblically significant is also strongly indicated by the years Steiner lectured upon them. His lecturing career spanned the first quarter of the twentieth century. Yet aside from his lectures starting in 1900 that culminated in his landmark book *Christianity as Mystical* *Fact*[4] in which he first identified Lazarus as Evangelist John, his focus upon the Bible virtually all occurred in the six plus years commencing in late 1907 and continuing through the end of 1913 when two concurring circumstances brought them to an end. The first and perhaps more potent of these was the imminent commencement of hostilities in 1914 producing conditions in the spiritual world that made further investigation in that domain implausible if not impossible. The second was his final departure from the Theosophical Society in 1913 as it in its Eastern-orientation became less and less hospitable to his Christology. It was between January 1911 and January 1912 when all six of these lectures were given, near the midst of this six-year span when he focused primarily upon the Bible. There

---

3. *(Continued from previous page)* The personality is to the individuality as the tip of an iceberg is to its far larger submerged portion. The personality is designed by the individuality and the heavenly hierarchies in the journey of the soul and spirit between incarnations, the purpose being to address a specific part of that individuality's accumulated karma or, in the case of more highly advanced in spiritual development, to act as a servant in addressing the karma of other beings.

4. Great Barrington, SteinerBooks, 2006.

were few lectures or writings during such period that fell outside that subject matter. Even those that might not seem on the
surface to be biblically related can in most instances upon careful inspection be seen to be so. Most notable is his *Outline of
Esoteric Science*, started earlier but published in late 1909. Few, if
any, of his works are so critical in comprehending the biblical
setting and content as that, even though its reach cannot be
limited thereto.

Between his final departure from the more Eastern-oriented
Theosophical Society in 1913 and the commencement of hostilities in 1914, Steiner entered upon a new phase of his mission
for humanity in which he felt it necessary that "Anthroposophy
spread more widely into general culture and civilization" and in
which his work expanded into other and more diverse disci-
plines. Yet it cannot be said that Steiner ever strayed from the
biblical connection for his life-changing epiphany in 1899
related to the Mystery of Golgotha and that most important
event in all creation was central to all he did thereafter.

Another phenomenon appears in holy writ that bears upon
this new edition. It has to do with the significance of a *name*. In
ancient times one's name or even the name of an item designated the very essence of its being or inherent nature, a spiritual reality no less. Today when we name a newborn child no
thought is given to this, nor is there generally the capability of
doing so. That was not the case in ancient times. As late as the
time of Christ it could still happen that names were so given,
though perhaps only by some fashion of atavistic insight no
longer common. We know, for instance, that the father of John
the Baptist was admonished by the angel of the Lord to name
his son John because of the nature of his spirit and of the mission he was to accomplish (Lk 1,8-23,57-64).

But the significance of the *name* becomes even more specifi-
cally relevant to the present publication because of what it
means in the case of the many name changes in the Bible.
Readily recognized are those such as Abram/Abraham, Sara/
Sarah, Jacob/Israel, Simon/Peter and Saul/Paul. Only with
Steiner can we now, with a reasonable confidence, put Laz-
arus/John in that group. In fact, that identification was given
in what might be called Steiner's debut into a specifically
Christian esotericism in his 1902 book *Christianity as Mystical
Fact*, as well as in his earliest Gospel lectures thereafter, those
on the Gospel of John.

But there is another more obscure name change that is perhaps the major impulse behind the present edition of this
book. When in 1988 at fifty-six years of age Rudolf Steiner
entered my life, or at least my consciousness in this life, I experienced the reality of a *turning point*. That year incidentally represented the transition year into my ninth and thus the last of
my predestined septenaries, in the way described above. At the
end of that last seven years the manuscript for my first book,
The Burning Bush,[5] was in process. One of its essays bears the
title "Widow's Son," an esoteric term of art. The focus of that
essay was the personality known in the book of Kings as both
Naboth and Elijah, for until Steiner it could hardly be known
that they were one and the same. Naboth was the personality's
name prior to his initiation into the mysteries of Mithra, Elijah the name given to him when initiated as described in the
book of Kings.

Much remains to be said about Elijah. In a most profound
way, we see that the individuality that incarnated in Naboth/

---

5. Great Barrington, Anthroposophic Press (SteinerBooks), 1997, rev. ed. 2001.

Elijah incarnated many times, as we all do, including as John the Baptist. Christ said of him, "Among those born of women none is greater than John" (Lk 7,28). We learn as we penetrate into Steiner's works that this individuality is the oldest in humanity, the first who was strong enough to remain embodied in matter as humanity was descending, the one we call Adam (or esoterically Adam Cadmon). It was from him that a part of his life body[6] was held back by the divine powers so as to remain unspoiled in the event known as "the fall." It was that preserved, unspoiled part that was divinely provided to the Jesus child in Luke's Gospel. This is what is behind the significance of the statement in that Gospel that when John's mother Elizabeth heard Mary's voice the babe in Elizabeth's womb "leaped" as if for joy that its unspoiled part was now incarnated (Lk 1,41). It is this same understanding that makes it possible to comprehend Paul's reference to the first and second Adam (1 Cor 15,45):

Thus it is written, "The first man Adam became a living being"; the last Adam became a life-giving spirit.

---

6. Anthroposophy shows that the human body is a composite that actually comprises three bodies, each uniquely related to one or more of the lower kingdoms. The way in which each of these came into existence from conditions of consciousness prior to the beginning of earth evolution is given in Steiner's *Outline of Esoteric Science* but can only be expressed here in extremely summary form. The oldest is the *physical* body which the human kingdom has in common with all the lower kingdoms. Next is the etheric or *life* body humanity holds in common with both the plant and animal kingdoms. The third component is the astral or *sense* body that humanity holds in common only with the animal kingdom. Only the human kingdom embodies an Ego or *I Am* consciousness, the element added by earth evolution. The existence of these three bodies is profusely demonstrated in holy scripture; see, for instance, the "Three Bodies" essay in *The Burning Bush*.

Nathan / Jesus

The "first Adam" was the one that descended as the first embodied human, while the "last Adam" was the one who received the unspoiled life body withheld from the first Adam when he descended. This understanding also begins to give meaning to the difference between the tree of life and the tree of knowledge in the Eden account.

Steiner's powerful revelations about this individuality are ably assembled and expounded by Sergei O. Prokofieff (grandson of the famous composer) in the early part of his book *Eternal Individuality*.[7]

But my motive for promoting this publication is focused even more intensely by the fact that, insofar as I am aware, the lecture in this volume that Steiner gave on Elijah (Berlin, December 14, 1911) is the only one in all his works, at least in those heretofore translated into English, that deals in any extensive way with this most exalted personality. A few months later (September 17, 1912 in Basel) in the third lecture of his cycle on Mark's Gospel, he spoke again of Elijah but only "briefly" noting that "I took advantage of the opportunity provided by the last general meeting of the German section of the Theosophical Society in Berlin to speak more fully on this subject."

The last English printing of *Turning Points in Spiritual History* was the Garber edition in 1987, which went out of print by the mid-nineties. Until I began writing this Introduction I was unaware of that edition, working myself from a machine-reproduced copy I made from the 1934 edition at the Rudolf Steiner Library. But from a point in the early nineties I have been among those strongly urging its republication by the Anthroposophic Press (now SteinerBooks). Its importance has

---

7. London, Temple Lodge, 1992 (first English edition).

long been recognized by this publisher, but a sort of triage necessitated by the allocation of resources in the face of an immense mission has kept it off the front burner. Finally, circumstances have conspired to end this delay and make this critical lecture available as part of the only English title in which it has yet appeared. It is to be noted that this publisher is presently engaged in the ambitious undertaking of getting all of Steiner's *Collected Works* (CW) into English print and keeping them there. These works are those found in his archives at the Goetheanum in Dornach, Switzerland, a suburb of Basel where they are known as *Gesamtausgabe* and referred to by GA number. The CW number in the English version will correspond with the GA number in the archives version. A complete list of all the *Collected Works* by number and descriptive title can be found at the back of the recently published *The Sun Mystery*.[8]

Certainly, this lecture on Elijah will eventually appear in CW 61. But there is sound reason for it appearing now in this present book because it is here placed in the unique context of a series of five personalities whose part in progressively preparing humanity for the Incarnation of the sixth is both profound and not widely appreciated. The importance of the deeply penetrating account of each of these important personalities being brought together into this one volume powerfully justifies its separate existence. It has to do with the great mystery of the Incarnation.

A brief digression will help to bring this out.

Steiner's name first came to my attention sometime in 1988 in Édouard Schuré's book *The Great Initiates*, NY, Harper & Row, 1961. It was originally published in Paris in 1889 but,

---

8. Great Barrington, SteinerBooks, 2006.

according to one recent source, has since gone through some 220 new editions and remains ever relevant. Paul M. Allen[9] wrote the introduction to the 1961 edition in which he stated:

> Of what Schuré called the three most significant friendships of his life, the first was with Richard Wagner, the second with Margherita Albana Mignaty, and the third [was] Rudolf Steiner.

It was clear that Steiner was the greatest of these three influences. Allen goes on to say:

> Through his friendship with Rudolf Steiner, for the first time in his life he found himself in the physical presence of a man whose spiritual stature and insight were akin to those figures he had described in his book. Therefore, in a certain sense, Schuré's relationship with Steiner was a kind of fulfillment of the spiritual-artistic task he had undertaken with the writing of *The Great Initiates*....

---

9. In his landmark work *Into the Heart's Land, A Century of Rudolf Steiner's Work in North America*, Henry Barnes frequently mentions the work of Paul Marshall Allen (1913-1998), and the entirety of his chapter 17, captioned "The First American-Born Anthroposophical Lecturer," is a biographical account of Allen provided by Allen's widow, Joan deRis Allen. Gene Gollogly also wrote an excellent biographical sketch, *In Memoriam*, to Allen in the Newsletter of the Anthroposophical Society shortly after the latter's death. Gollogly had also suggested to me earlier after *The Burning Bush* was published that I should call Paul Allen who then lived in Aberdeen, Scotland, giving me his phone number. Again, I delayed for a considerable period of time before one day following through on that. A wonderfully rewarding conversation occurred. It was only weeks after that when news came of his death. It was my good fortune to meet and dine with his widow Joan, who now lives at Kimberton, PA, at the Anthroposophical Conference 2005 in Ann Arbor, MI.

In May, 1906, Édouard Schuré and Rudolf Steiner met for the first time when the latter visited Paris to give a course of eighteen lectures on matters of spiritual knowledge. Schuré recalled that: "From all I had heard from Marie von Sivers and had read elsewhere, I had indeed expected a man who might have the same goal as myself. However, I was rather indifferent when Rudolf Steiner came to meet me.

"Then—as he stood in the doorway and looked at me with eyes which revealed an understanding of infinite heights and depths of development, and his almost ascetic countenance, expressing and instilling kindness and boundless confidence—he made a tremendous impression upon me (*une impression foudroyante*). Such an impression I had experienced only twice before in my life, and then much less strongly, with Richard Wagner and with Margherita Albana Mignaty. Immediately two things became clear to me, even before Rudolf Steiner started to speak.

"For the very first time I was certain that an initiate stood before me. For a long while I had lived in spirit with initiates of the past, whose history and development I had attempted to describe. And here at last, one stood before me on the physical plane."

But it was what was said even later in Allen's introduction that impelled me to find out more about this man. Even so, it was a few months before I got around to checking him out, so that it was February, 1989 before I got my first Steiner book, *The Course of My Life* (now his *Autobiography*).[10] Thence charmed,

---

10. Great Barrington, Anthroposophic Press, 1999.

I began the furious and voracious study of his works bearing most directly upon the Bible until in 1994 I began to write *The Burning Bush.*

Thus prefaced, it is worth noting the eight initiates about whom Schuré writes, Rama, Krishna, Hermes, Moses, Orpheus, Pythagoras, Plato and Jesus. In no way is it suggested that Schuré's book should be measured against Steiner's or against the whole of Steiner's work. It is, in fact, remarkable that seventeen years before he met Steiner he was able to write such a book, coming out of the spiritualism of the 19th century. He was largely inspired in the effort by Margherita Albana Mignaty. Steiner wrote an introduction for a 1909 German edition in which he stated that Schuré traced "the great spiritual deeds of Rama, Krishna, Hermes, Pythagoras and Plato, in order to show the unification of all these impulses in Christ."

Indeed, one could say that Schuré succeeded in this endeavor. Since both Schuré and Steiner concluded with the Christ, thus each fashioning the entirety of his book as a thread paving humanity's way to the Christ, why was there so little overlap in personalities? Only Hermes and Moses were common to the preparatory thread. And Steiner himself had said that Christianity was the fulfillment of all true religions, and had himself spoken of all those initiates except perhaps Rama by name, but certainly even of him insofar as his period in human development was concerned. And certainly those initiates Schuré covered could be said to represent "turning points in spiritual history" from many perspectives.

Why then their different selections? The distinction lay in the fact that every one of those selected by Marie von Sivers Steiner not only represented such a "great initiate" and "turning point," but also one who was most significantly and critically involved in the preparation of the body and/or person (soul) of Jesus of Nazareth; cf. "A body hast thou prepared for me" (Heb 10,5). Here we enter the realm of the Nativity, and in that account we distinguish between Jesus of Nazareth and Jesus Christ, the baptism of Jesus being the point at which Jesus of Nazareth became Jesus Christ, signified scripturally by the descent of the dove in all four canonical Gospels. We can point only in summary form toward all these underlying indications, but it is important to understand that it is in this great mystery that the distinction lay.

The order of appearance of these five preparatory personalities is only partially chronological. Their names in chronological order are Zarathustra, Hermes, Moses, Elijah and Buddha. This is slightly different from the order designated by Marie Steiner for the original publication. Whatever her reason for that order, it is honored herein. It is noted that those who are ostensibly part of the biblical lineage of the Hebrew people are listed chronologically (i.e., Moses and Elijah), but are given immediately before the Christ lecture. Those not part of that same lineage (Zarathustra, Hermes and Buddha) are listed first. But in truth, all five are involved in the biblical account leading up to the Incarnation of Christ, as we shall see.

We will leave it to the lectures themselves to otherwise sufficiently reveal these five personalities. It is the presumed reason for their inclusion here to which our immediate attention is directed, namely, the unique part each played in the long process of preparing an earthly human body spiritually powerful enough to receive in the flesh the searing power of the Christ Spirit, the great Sun Spirit, Ahura Mazdao or Ormuzd, that the ancient Zarathustra had seen in the sun's aura.

The earliest of the five is Zarathustra. The name is Persian, in Greek it is Zoroaster. Its literal meaning is shining or lustrous star, a most appropriate designation both as to its ancient bearer and as to its appearance at the birth of the Jesus child in Matthew's Gospel. Also to be noted is that the Zarathustra here involved lived several thousand years before Christ, though his *individuality* appeared again in another personality with the same name (Zoroaster, or Zarathas or Nazarathos) when he was again in the region but this time in Babylon where it is said that he taught Pythagoras and also the middle-period Hebrew prophets such as Second Isaiah and Ezekiel. Does this not prompt a deep pondering as one reads the suffering-servant prophecies in Second Isaiah?

Those readers may be initially disconcerted by the account of the two Jesus children, at least until they see how extensively it comports with the two biblical accounts, more so than any other attempt at reconciliation of the two versions since the time of Christ, versions otherwise widely recognized as incompatible by most biblical scholars. Matthew's account (Mt 1–2) tells of the child descended from David's son Solomon (Mt 1,6) known as the "Solomon Jesus" child; Luke's account (Lk 1–2 and 3,23-38) tells of the one descended[11] from David's son Nathan (Lk 3,31) known as the "Nathan Jesus" child. Luke's account alone reports the only incident in Jesus's life between the nativity and the three years of his ministry starting

---

11. Respectively, Great Barrington, Anthroposophic Press, 2001 (10 lectures, Basel, Sept. 1909) and Great Barrington, Anthroposophic Press, 4th Ed., 1965 (10 lectures, Berne, Sept. 1910). An unpublished lecture (November 14, 1909) available only in typescript at the Rudolf Steiner Library, Ghent, NY is also a most helpful supplement; see *The Gospels*, Anthroposophic News Sheet, Dornach, Switzerland.

thirty years[12] later (Lk 2,41-51). Its significance lay in the fact that it tells of the event when the two Jesus children, previously neighbors in Nazareth, and of quite different nature, became one—Jesus of Nazareth. Luke's Gospel, written by one closely associated with Paul (who alone spoke of the "first and second Adam"), contains many other priceless indicators about the Incarnation that are not found in Matthew. One of those is his giving the genealogy only at the point in his account where Jesus had been baptized and the Christ Spirit had descended as a "dove" alighting upon Jesus. The Incarnation was completed only at that time, whence Jesus of Nazareth truly became Jesus Christ. Although much early and medieval art can be seen to disclose the two Jesus children, the hand of providence can be seen in waiting for two thousand years before the more complete story could be fleshed out by an initiate of the highest order. Notably the end of that waiting period coincided, according to Steiner, with the end in 1899 of the five thousand year age of darkness known in the Orient as Kali Yuga. The present lectures do not give the story of those two children, but they do deal with those personalities that were directly involved in the very being of the two. One who comprehends the Nativity as thus presented must necessarily come away impressed with the extent to which the Incarnation was a work of the spiritual world over a long period of preparation, and how its "great light" came, as the scriptures say, at the "right time." But Zarathustra's significance is not thus exhausted. Here we enter upon esoteric matters of great profundity. Only

---

12. Smith, Great Barrington, Anthroposophic Press, 1998. Also, for those with perhaps some prior grounding in Anthroposophy, an incomparably beautiful account is given in Emil Bock's *The Childhood of Jesus, The Unknown Years*, Edinburgh, Floris Books, 1997.

a highly condensed synopsis can be given, designed to point to the reason for the selections, but otherwise inadequate for the more inquisitive reader. The underlying details are to be found in two of Steiner's lecture cycles. Foremost of the two is *According to Luke* (especially lectures three through five), while vitally supplemental to it is *The Gospel of St. Matthew* (especially lectures two and three). Readers not already familiar with Steiner's insights into Christ's nativity may also find helpful "The Nativity" essay in *The Burning Bush*, as well as its more popular-style version in *The Incredible Birth's of Jesus*.

Zarathustra was the primary initiate of the second cultural era, what Steiner calls the Persian, following Noah's expedition upon the final submergence of the ancient Atlantis, the fourth of the great epochs of earth evolution. The Persian era or age followed the ancient Indian and preceded the Chaldo-Egyptian, which itself preceded the Greco-Roman. Each such age corresponded with a zodiacal period of approximately 2,160 years, to put matters in perspective. Our present European age commenced at the time of the Renaissance, the Greco-Roman at the time that First Isaiah noted the coming end of the ability to see, hear or understand the spiritual realm (Is 6). And the Chaldo-Egyptian commenced with the age of writing nearly three millennia before Christ. So our ancient Zarathustra lived in the age considered prehistorical.

Zarathustra then reincarnated many additional times, and in many differing locales, before his "star" descended as the Ego, the "I Am," of the Solomon Jesus child in Matthew's Gospel, leading his spiritual descendants, the Zoroastrian magi of Persia, to the child's birthplace in Bethlehem. The hand of providence preserved for two thousand years many works thought to have been destroyed as Christendom coalesced over the first four centuries into the dogma of the Roman Church. Only after that period of time was Christendom ready to again look more closely at the early Christians following the deaths of those who had known the earthly Christ. Near the middle of the twentieth century numerous works of those early years were unearthed in the collection found at Nag Hammadi in Egypt. Among those was one called *The Apocalypse of Adam.* Oxford Fellow Andrew Welburn, in his *The Book with Fourteen Seals*, has given us a marvelous explication of how this Essene takes us through the incarnations of Zarathustra prior to his incarnation as the soul (Ego) of the Solomon Jesus child.[13] In each of the first twelve of those incarnations it is said of him, "And thus he came on the water," so reminiscent of what is said of the birth of Moses.

By the time the ancient soul of Zarathustra entered the Solomon Jesus child, it could properly be said that he had assimilated more of what the cultures of humanity had provided than any other soul or individuality and was thus the wisest of all. The Nathan Jesus child, during his first twelve years, had an etheric body that had not experienced "the fall" and was thus pure, as was his astral body. These served sufficiently as a "provisional Ego" for this child during his first twelve years. He was, of all creatures, the most sensitive to nature and the most compassionate toward all its creatures, but entirely naive in a worldly way. Through a process known to the initiates from the ancient mysteries, as had often happened, the soul of one person slips out of his or her three bodies and into those of another human being. In this case the Zarathustra Ego entered the three bodies of the Nathan Jesus

---

13. Sussex, Rudolf Steiner Press, 1991.

child, thus bringing to this child all the accumulated wisdom of ages past. This is what makes understandable the fact that his parents were so astonished with his ability to confound the savants in the temple when he was only twelve years old. The majesty of this one event, the twelve-year-old event, is why it is the only thing of critical importance that had to be told of the first thirty years after the Nativity. Thence this boy grew and matured as Jesus of Nazareth. And it was this great Zarathustra soul, the one who must surely have taught Second Isaiah, who sacrificed himself, withdrawing at the time of his baptism for the entry of the Christ Spirit and its three-years as Jesus Christ.

Zarathustra was also a critical instrumentality in two of the other intervening personalities, Hermes and Moses. To bring about a threefold body sufficiently perfected to receive the Zarathustra soul or Ego in its most critical incarnation, a special people were needed, a people often called in biblical terminology a "chosen people." It was necessary that this people be kept pure for the development of the appropriate human sheaths or bodies, physical, etheric and astral—bodies that would be capable of receiving and containing the great Christ Spirit for three years. Unsullied blood descent was vital to this goal, hence we see endogamous marriage from the time of Abraham in the lineage of the Jesus children. The setting for this lineage is in the Chaldo-Egyptian age, and it is here that Zarathustra additionally makes his mark through his two most intimate pupils. One of these incarnated later as Hermes, the founder of Egyptian culture with its sun wisdom, and the other as Moses who took what was needed from that culture and carried it forward into the people that came to be known as the chosen people, a moon people.

Still the influence of Zarathustra does not end there. In his lecture cycle on Matthew's Gospel, Steiner shows how it is Zarathustra's wisdom that made its way through Hermes and Moses and then finally through the great teacher of the Essenes (Jeshu ben Pandira) into the lineage or genealogy of the Jesus child in Matthew's Gospel. We see there how fourteen generations are needed for the perfection of each of the three bodies, comprising forty-two generations in total from the time of Abraham. Little wonder that it is Persian initiates who appear as magi who saw this great soul descend as a star into the Jesus child in Matthew's Gospel. Moreover, Jeshu ben Pandira, the great Essene teacher, had five pupils, two of whom were especially significant in the appearance of Jesus of Nazareth. It is from one named Netzer that the Nazirites derived, of which the little community of Nazareth was composed. And from one named Matthai came the teaching upon which the forty-two generations was based and for whom the Gospel of Matthew was named.

We've seen how Hermes and Moses were both involved in the formation of the Hebrew ancestry that was essential in the development of the physical bodies of both Jesus children. The other two personalities between Zarathustra and Christ, namely Buddha and Elijah, are intimately involved in or with the etheric and astral bodies of the Nathan Jesus child. It is in Steiner's lecture cycle on Luke's Gospel that we learn of these.

We've already noted the special relationship between the etheric (life) bodies of the Nathan Jesus child and John the Baptist, who was the reincarnated Elijah and many ages before that was Adam. We saw how the unspoiled life body in the newly-conceived Nathan Jesus fetus quickened the six-month old fetus of John the Baptist in Elizabeth's womb so that it jumped when

Adam → Elijah → John the Baptist

it heard Mary's greeting to Elizabeth. These two infants were essentially soul mates. It is notable that while Matthew's genealogy for the Solomon Jesus child included only the forty-two generations from Abraham and preceded the account of the child's birth, Luke's included seventy-seven generations back through Adam to God. Moreover, this genealogy is not given until after the account of the twelve-year old Jesus in the temple and the baptism of Jesus and the descent of the Christ Spirit upon him. The ancient connection of John the Baptist and the Nathan Jesus child is thus powerfully shown. They are indeed the first and second Adam, as Paul describes them.

There remains only Buddha to weave into this line-up, and he is intricately interwoven in it. Steiner tells us that the mission of Gautama Buddha was to incorporate into humanity the principle of compassion and love. Prior to his time love came through blood relationship. The Buddha attained perfection of his astral body to the extent possible at that time in human evolution. The Oriental term for a perfected astral body is *nirmanakaya*. Steiner tells us that it was this nirmanakaya of Buddha that appeared to the shepherds in the field in Luke's Gospel and also became the astral body of the Nathan Jesus child in Mary's womb and along with that child's pure life body quickened the soul of the child in Elizabeth's womb.

It is said of the righteous and devout Simeon, who when the parents brought the infant Jesus to the temple according to the custom of the law took the infant up in his arms and blessed him saying, "Lord, now lettest thou thy servant depart in peace ... for mine eyes have seen thy salvation," that he Simeon was the reincarnated Asita, the wise man who had recognized the infant Gautama as the Bodhisattva at his birth and now recognized his former master in the infant Jesus child.

In many ways Steiner indicated over the course of his mission that the Incarnation of the Christ was the fulfillment of all true religions. Christendom as a mere religion can hardly fully appropriate the Christ who came for all of creation. Christianity in its true sense is for all. In Stuttgart, on November 14, 1909, in a lecture entitled *The Gospels*, Steiner said:

In Christ Jesus we really have a fusion and at the same time a rebirth of all the former spiritual streams of humanity. In Him the earlier streams are born anew, in an enhanced degree. We could mention many such streams belonging to pre-Christian times ... spiritual streams which all flow into the Christ Event and there unite."

The personalities featured in this volume are those who, coming out of and indeed founding earlier religions down through the ages, cooperated vitally with the powers in the spiritual world to bring about the Incarnation of the Christ, the most important event in all creation. Indeed, each was clearly a *turning point in spiritual history.*

1. ZARATHUSTRA

[handwritten: Persian]
[handwritten: Solomon - Jesus]
[handwritten: Matthew Gospel]

AMONG the fundamental principles underlying spiritual science and to which your attention has been drawn in previous lectures, the most prominent is the idea of reincarnation. According to this generally unpopular and little understood concept, it is maintained that human individuality is con- *[handwritten: single earthly incarnation]* strained to manifest again and again in a single personality during its unfoldment in the course of repeated earth lives. It has been pointed out previously that many and diverse questions are associated with this concept, and this will become more and more apparent as we proceed.

What deep meaning, we might ask, underlies the fact that the span of a person's life on the earth is destined to recur not once only but many times and that during each successive period between rebirth and death the human individuality persists. *[handwritten: The ego or I am that keeps incarnating over + over]* When we study the evolution of humankind in the light of spiritual science, we find therein a progressive meaning, a design of such nature that each age and each epoch presents in some fashion a different content. We realize that human evolution is ever destined to maintain a definite upward trend. Thus do we become aware of a profound latent significance, when we know that the varied influences that act upon humankind are indeed potent and become absorbed over and over again by the

"I" during the course of human development. This is possible only because a person's essential being is brought into contact not once alone but recurrently with the great living stream of evolution. When we regard the whole evolutionary process as a rational progression, ever accompanied by fresh contents, there dawns a true comprehension of those great spiritual beings who set the measure of progress. We are then able to realize the import and proper relationship of these outstanding leaders, from whom have come new thoughts, experiences, and impulses destined to further the advancement and progressive evolution of humanity.

During this cycle of lectures I shall speak of many such spiritual beings who have acted as guides to humankind and at the same time bring forward and elucidate various matters connected with this subject. The first human individuality to claim our attention from such a point of view is Zarathustra, about whom little is known, though there is much discussion in these days. For as far as external investigation goes, his history is especially difficult to fathom, as it is shrouded in mystery and unrecorded in ancient documents. When we consider the characteristics of such a personality as Zarathustra, whose gifts to humankind as far as they are preserved for us, seem so strange to our present age, we at once realize how great is the dissimilarity in the human's whole being at different periods of earthly progress. Casual reflection might easily lead to the conclusion that from the very beginning humanity has always had the same ideas concerning morality, the same general thoughts, feelings, and conceptions as those that exist in our time. From previous lectures, however, and from others that will follow, you will know through the teachings of spiritual science that during humankind's development great and important changes take place, especially with respect to the life of the human soul, the nature of human apprehension, emotions, and desires. Further, you will realize that humanity's consciousness was very differently constituted in olden days and that there is reason to believe that in the future yet other stages will be reached in which the conscious condition of humankind will vary considerably from its normal state today.

When we turn our attention to Zarathustra, we find that we must look back over an extremely long period of time. According to certain modern researches, he is considered to be a contemporary of Buddha, the approximate date of his life being fixed at some six to six and a half centuries before the birth of Christianity. It is, however, a remarkable and interesting fact that other investigators of late years, after carefully studying all existing traditions concerning Zarathustra, have been driven to the conclusion that the personality concealed beneath the name of the ancient founder of the Persian religion must have lived a great many centuries before the time of Buddha. Greek historians have stated over and over again that the period ascribed to Zarathustra should be put back very many years, possibly five to six thousand years before the Trojan War [the date of which has been placed at about 1200 B.C.E.].

In this light and from what has been learned through research in many directions, we can now feel certain that historical investigators will in the end be unwillingly forced to acknowledge that the claims of Grecian scholarship regarding the great antiquity of the Zarathustran era, as indicated by ancient tradition, are justly founded and must be accepted as authentic. In its statements and theories, spiritual science fully concurs with the old Greek writers who in olden days fixed the period of the founder of the Persian religion so far back in

6,000 BC

time. We have, therefore, good reason for maintaining that Zarathustra, living as he did thousands of years before the birth of Christianity, was doubtless confronted with a very different class of human consciousness from that which exists in our present age.

It has often been pointed out, and we will again refer to this matter, that in ancient times the development of human consciousness was such that the old "dream state," or "clairvoyant condition" (we will avoid misusing this term, as is so often done these days), was in every way perfectly normal to human beings, so that their conceptions and ideas were such that they did not contemplate the world from that narrow perceptual point of view that is so prevalent today. We can best picture the impressions made by the world upon the consciousness of the ancients if we turn our thoughts to that last enduring remnant of the old clairvoyant state, namely, dream consciousness. We all know those fluctuating dream pictures that come to us at times, the most of which carry no meaning and are so often merely suggestive of the outer world, though there may now and then intrude some higher level of conscious thought— dream visions, which at the present time we find so difficult to interpret and to understand. We might say that our sleep consciousness runs its course pictorially in ever-changing scenes, which are at the same time symbolic. For instance, many of us have had the experience that events connected with some impressive happening—say, a conflagration—have been after a time once more figuratively manifested to us in a dream. Let us now consider for a moment this other horizon of our sleeping state, where clings in truth that last remnant of a conscious condition belonging to a bygone age in the gray and distant past.

The consciousness of the ancients was such that in reality they lived in a life of imagery. The visions that came to them were not merely indefinite, unrelated creations, for they had reference to an actual outer world. In olden days human beings were capable of intermediate conscious states, between those that prevail when we sleep and when we are awake; then it was that they lived in the presence of the spirit world, and the spirit world entered into their being. Today this door is closed, but in those ancient times such was not the case. It was while they were in this intermediate condition that humans became aware of visions that resembled to some extent dream pictures but were definite in their manifestation of a spirit life and of spiritual achievement existing beyond the perceptual world. Although in the Zarathustran era such visions had become somewhat confused and vague, there was nevertheless still close contact with the world of spirit. Thus, these ancients could say from direct observation and experience: "In the same way that I realize this outer physical world and this perceptual life, even so do I *know* that there exists another conscious condition belonging to a different region—a spiritual realm—related to that which is material and where I do truly experience and observe the workings of the Divine Spirit."

It is a fundamental principle underlying the evolution of the human race that in no case can any one quality be developed except at the expense of some other attribute; hence it came about that from epoch to epoch the faculty through which in olden times humankind obtained a clear inner vision of the spiritual realms became less and less pronounced. Our present-day exact methods of thought, our power of expression, our logic, and all that we regard as the most important driving forces of modern culture did not exist in the remote past. Such faculties have been acquired during later periods at the expense of the old clairvoyant consciousness, and it is now for human-kind to regain and cultivate this long-lost power. Then, in the future of human evolution, a time will come when in addition to human beings' purely physical consciousness, intellectuality and logic, they will again approach the condition of the ancient seer.

We must differentiate between the upward and downward tendency of human consciousness. Evolution has a deeper meaning when we realize that in the beginning human beings were entirely of a spiritual realm, where they lived in the soul; when they descended into the physical world, it was ordained that they should gradually relinquish clairvoyant power in order to acquire qualities born of the existing purely physical conditions, such as intellectuality and logic. When this stage in their development has run its course, human beings will again return to the world of spirit.

Regarding the circumstances connected with these curious clairvoyant states and experiences of the ancients we have no historical record. Zarathustra lived in that same remote age and was one of those great leading personalities who gave immense stimulus to the advancement of culture and civilization. Such guiding personalities must ever draw from the creative source that which we may term Illumination, whereby they are initi-ated into the higher mysteries of the world irrespective of the standard of normal human consciousness existing in their time. Other such outstanding personalities of whom mention will be made during these lectures are Hermes, Buddha, and Moses. Zarathustra lived at least eight thousand years before the present era, and those glorious gifts to civilization that emanated from his illumined spirit have been reflected in the great cultural progress of humanity. His influence has long ago been clearly recognized and can be detected even to this day by all who take note of the mysterious currents underlying the whole of human evolution.

We now realize that Zarathustra belonged essentially to those great ones in whose souls lived a measure of the spiritual elements of truth, wisdom, and perception, far surpassing the customary standard of human consciousness of their period. His mission was to proclaim to his fellow human beings, in that part of the world later known as the Persian Empire, the grand truths that emanated from the superperceptual regions—a world utterly beyond the apprehension of normal human consciousness in that dim and distant age. If we would understand the true significance of Zarathustra's teachings, we must remember that it was his task to present to a certain section of humanity, in an intelligible manner, a particular world aspect. At the same time, various movements in progress among the peoples of other regions of the world had imparted a different trend to the whole sphere of human culture.

The personality of Zarathustra is of special interest, because he lived in a territory, contiguous upon its southern side to a country inhabited by Indian ethnic groups, upon whom spiritual blessings flowed in quite a different manner. When we look forward from those bygone times, we find upon the same soil where these ancient Indian groups lived, the peoples among whom at a later period arose the poets of the Vedas. To the north, where the great Brahman doctrine developed, is situated the region that was permeated throughout by the powerful and compelling teachings of Zarathustra. But that which he gave to the world was in many respects fundamentally different from the teachings of the great leaders among the Indians, whose words have lived on in the moving poetry of the Vedas and in their profound philosophy and found an echo in that final glorious blaze of light—the revelation of the Buddha.

We can understand the difference between that which was born of the flow of thought from Zarathustra and the teachings of the ancient Indians when we bear in mind that we can approach the region of the superperceptual world from two sides. In other lectures we have spoken of the path that human beings must traverse in order to enter into the spirit realms. There are two possible methods by which they may raise the energy of their souls and the capacities latent in their inner beings so much above their normal level that they can pass out of this perceptual world into the superperceptual world. First, human beings can retire more and more deeply into the soul and thus merge themselves in their very essence. The second method leads behind the veil spread around us by our material state. Human beings can enter the superperceptual region by both these methods.

When we experience within our very being a deepening of all values of our spiritual feelings, conceptions, and ideas—in short, of our soul impulses—and when, in fact, we creep more and more into ourselves so that our spiritual powers become ever stronger and stronger, then can we in some mystic way merge ourselves within and pass through all that we hold of the physical world to our actual spirit essence, to the soul "I" that continues from incarnation to incarnation and is not perishable but everlasting. When we have overcome our lusts and passions and all those experiences of the soul that are ours because we are of the body in a physical world, then can our true being pierce the surrounding veil and forever enter the world of spirit.

On the other hand, if we develop those powers that will enable us not merely to be sensible of the outer world with its colors, tone sensations, heat and cold, and if we so strengthen our spiritual forces that we shall be aware of that which lies beyond the colors, the sound, the heat and the cold, and all those other earthly sense perceptions that hang as a mist about us, then will the enhanced powers of our soul take us behind the enshrouding cloud and into that boundless superperceptual region that is without confine and stretches ever into the infinite.

There is one way leading to the spirit world that we may term the "mystical method" and another that is properly called "the method of spiritual science." All great spiritual personalities have followed these paths in order to attain to those truths and revelations that it was their mission to impress upon humanity in the form of cultural progress. In primeval times the human being's development was of such a nature that great revelations could come only to the people of any particular race through *one* of these methods alone. But from that period in which the Greeks lived onward—that is, at the dawn of the Christian era—these two separate thought currents commingled and became more and more one single cultural stream. When we now speak of entering the higher spheres, we understand that those who would penetrate into the superperceptual region develop *both* qualities of power in the soul. The forces necessary to the mystical method are evolved within the inner being, and those essential to the course of spiritual science are strengthened while the human being is yet conscious of the outer world. There is today no longer any definite separation of these two paths, because these two currents have run their course together since about the time of that epoch marked by the life of the Grecian race. In the one, revelation comes about through a mystic merging of consciousness within a person's very being; in the other, the veil is torn asunder by the enhanced power of an individual's spiritual forces, and a person's awareness stretches outward into the great cosmos.

In olden times, before the Grecian or Christian era, these two possible methods were in operation separately among different peoples, and we find them working in close proximity but in divers ways in the Indian culture that found expression among the Vedas, on the one hand, and that of Zarathustra, further north, on the other. All that we look upon with such wonder in the ancient Indian culture and that later found expression through Buddha was achieved by inner contemplation and turning away from the outer world through causing the eyes to become less sensitive to physical colors and the ears to physical sounds and bringing about a deadening of the sense organs in general to the perceptual veil, so that the inner soul forces might be strengthened. Thus did humanity press on to Brahma, there to feel unified with that which ever works and weaves as the Inner Spirit of the universe. In this way originated the teachings of the Holy Rishis, which live on in the poetry of the Vedas, in the Vedantic philosophy, and in Buddhism.

The doctrine of Zarathustra was, however, entirely based upon the other method mentioned. He taught his disciples the secret of strengthening their powers of apprehension and cognition that they might pass beyond the mists surrounding the outer perceptual world. He did not say to his followers, as did the Indian teachers, "Turn away from the colors and from the sounds and from all outer sense impressions and seek the path to the spiritual realms only through the merging of yourselves within your very souls." Instead, he spoke thus: "Strengthen

[margin annotation: inward enlightenment]

[bottom annotation: outward enlightenment]

your powers of perception so that you may look around upon
all things—the plants, the animals, that which lives in the air
and in the water, upon the mountains, and in the depths of the
valleys—and cast your eyes upon the world." We know that
the disciples of the Indian mystics regarded this earth upon
which we live as merely maya [illusion], and turned from it in
order to attain to Brahma. On the other hand, Zarathustra
counseled his followers *not* to draw away from the material
world but to pass outward and beyond it, so that they might
say, "Whenever we experience perceptual manifestations in the
outer physical world, we realize that therein lie concealed and
beyond our sense perceptions the workings and achievements
of the spirit."

It is remarkable that the two paths should have been thus
united in early Grecian times. Just because in that period true
spiritual knowledge was more profound than in our day (which
we are inclined to regard as so amazingly enlightened!), all
things found expression in imagery, and the images gave rise to
mythology. Thus do we find these two thought currents
commingled and fostered in the Grecian culture—the mystical
tending inward and the Zarathustran outward into the great
cosmos.

That such was the case becomes evident from the fact that
one of these paths was named after Dionysus, that mysterious
god who was reached when human beings merged ever deeper
and deeper within their inner being, there to find a
questionable subhuman element, as yet unknown, and from
which they first developed. It was this unclean and half-animal
residue to which was given the name of Dionysus. On the
other hand, all that comes to us when we regard our physical
sense perceptions from a purely spiritual standpoint was

termed Apollo. Thus in ancient Greece we find side by side, in contrast, the teaching of Zarathustra in the Apollo current of thought and the doctrine of mystical contemplation in the Dionysus current. In Greece they united and operated conjointly—the Zarathustran and the mystical methods, those methods that had been at their highest level yet working separately in the days of the ancient Indians.

Here we might say that in olden times these two thought currents were destined to commingle in the coming Grecian cults of Apollo and Dionysus, and thenceforward they would continue as one, so that in our present cultural period, when we raise ourselves to a certain spiritual understanding, we find them still unified and enduring.

It is very remarkable and one of the many riddles that present themselves to the thinking mind that Nietzsche in his first work, *The Birth of Tragedy from the Spirit of Music*, gave evidence of a vague suspicion that in the Grecian creeds of Dionysus and Apollo the mystical current meets the stream of scientific-spiritual thought.

A further matter of interest lies in the fact that Zarathustra actually taught his disciples to recognize in detail the hidden workings of the spirit in all material things, and from this starting point the whole of his gifts to culture emanated. He emphasized that it was not sufficient for humankind merely to say: "There before us spreads a material world, behind which ever works and weaves the Divine Spirit." Such a statement might appear at first sight full of significance, but it leads only to a general pantheistic outlook and means nothing more than that some vague nebulous spirit underlies all material phenomena. Zarathustra, like all other great personalities of the past who were exalted and had direct contact with the spirit world, did not present these matters to his followers and the people in any such indefinite and abstract manner; he pointed out that in the same way as individual physical happenings vary in import, so is it with the latent spiritual factor, it being sometimes of greater and sometimes of lesser moment. He further stated that the sun, regarded purely from the physical point of view as a member of the stellar system, is the source of all earthly phenomena, life, and activity, while concealed within is the center of spiritual existence insofar as we are immediately concerned.

These things Zarathustra impressed earnestly and clearly upon his disciples. Using simple words, we can picture him as addressing them somewhat as follows: "When you regard human beings, you must realize that they do not consist only of a material body—this is but an outer expression of the spirit that is within. Even as the physical covering is a manifestation in condensed and crystallized form of the true spiritual human being, so is the sun that appears to us as a light-giving mass, when considered as such, merely the external manifestation of an inner spiritual sun." In the same way as we term the human spirit element, as distinguished from the physical, the Aura, to use an ancient expression, so do we call the all-embracing hidden spiritual part of the sun, the Great Aura (Aura Mazda), in contradistinction to the human being's spiritual component, which is sometimes called the Little Aura. Zarathustra named all that lies hidden within and beyond the human being's mere apprehension of the physical sun "Aura Mazda" or "Ahura Mazdao" and considered this element as important to our spiritual experiences and conditions, as is the physical sun to the well-being of plants and animals and all that lives upon the face of the earth. There behind the physical sun lies the Spiritual Master, the Creator, "Ahura Mazdao" or *outward*

"Aura Mazda"; from "Ahura Mazdao" came the name "Ormuzd," or "the Spirit of Light."

inward

While the Indians mystically searched their inner being to attain to Brahma—the Eternal—who shines outward as a point of light from within the human essence, Zarathustra urged his disciples to turn their eyes upon the great periphery of existence and pointed out that there within the body of the sun dwells the great Solar Spirit—Ahura Mazdao, "the Spirit of Light." He taught them that in the same way as human beings strive to raise their spirit to perfection, so must they ever battle against the lower passions and desires, against the delusive images suggested by possible deception and falsehood and all those antagonistic influences within, which continually oppose spiritual impulses. Thus must Ahura Mazdao face the opposition of "the Spirit of Darkness—"Angra Mainyus," or "Ahriman."

Ahriman

We can now realize how the great Zarathustran conception could evolve from experiences born of sensations and sense contents. Through them, Zarathustra could advance his disciples to a point where he could make clear to them that within human beings there is a "Perfecting Principle" that tells them that whatever may be their present condition, this principle will work persistently within and that through it they may raise ever higher and higher; at the same time, however, there also operate impulses and inclinations, deceit and falsehood, all tending toward imperfection. This Perfecting Principle must therefore be developed and expanded so that the world may be destined to attain to wiser and more advanced states of perfection; it is the "Principle of Ahura Mazdao," and it is assailed throughout the whole world by Ahriman—the Spirit of Darkness—who through imperfection and evil brings shadows into the light. By following the method outlined, Zarathustra's disciples were enabled to realize and to feel that in truth each individual human being is an image of the outer universe.

We must not seek the true significance of such teaching in theories, concepts, and ideas but in active, vivid consciousness and in the sensations impressed when through them human beings realize that they are so related to the universe that they can say: "As I stand here, I am a small world, and as such I am a replica of the Great Cosmos." Just as we have within us a principle of perfection and another that is antagonistic, so throughout the universe is Ormuzd opposed by Ahriman. In these teachings the whole cosmos is represented as typical of a widespread human being; the forces of greatest virtue are termed Ahura Mazdao, while against these operate the powers of Angra Mainyus.

When human beings realize that they are in direct contact with the workings of the universe and the attendant physical phenomena but can apprehend only the perceptual, then, as they begin to gain spiritual experience, a feeling of awe may come over them (especially if they are materialistic in thought) when they learn through spectrum analysis that the same matter that exists upon the earth is found in the most distant stars. It is the same with Zarathustranism, when human beings feel that their spiritual part is merged in that of the whole cosmos and that they have indeed emanated from its great spirit. Herein lies the true significance of such a doctrine, which was not merely abstract in character but wholly concrete.

In the present age it is most difficult to make people understand (even when they have a certain sense for the spiritual that lies behind the perceptual) that it is necessary to a true and spiritually scientific view of the cosmos that there be more than one central unity of spirit power. Even as we distinguish between the separate forces in nature, such as heat, light, and chemical forces, so in the world of spirit must we not merely recognize one centralized power (whose existence is not denied) but also differentiate between it and certain subservient uplifting forces whose spheres of action are more circumscribed than are those of the all-embracing spirit. Thus it was that Zarathustra made a distinction between the omnipotent Ormuzd and those spirit beings by whom he was served.

Before we turn to a consideration of these subservient spirit entities, we must draw attention to the fact that the Zarathustran theory was not a mere dualism, a simple doctrine of two worlds—the worlds of Ormuzd and of Ahriman—but that it maintained that underlying this double flux of cosmic influence is a definite unity, a single power, which gave birth to both "the Realm of Light" (Ormuzd) and "the Realm of Darkness" (Ahriman). It is not easy to gain a right understanding of Zarathustra's conception concerning this "Unity" underlying Ormuzd and Ahriman. With reference to this point the Greek authors state that the ancient Persians worshipped and regarded as a "Living Unity" that which lay beyond the light and which Zarathustra termed "Zervane Akarene." How can we gain a comprehension of what Zarathustra in his teachings meant by "Zervane Akarene" or "Zaruana Akarana"?

Let us consider for a moment the course of evolution; this we must regard as of such nature that all beings tend toward greater and greater perfection. If we look into the future, we see more and more of the radiance from the light realms of Ormuzd; but if we turn our eyes upon the past, we realize how the powers of Ahriman, which oppose Ormuzd, are there. We then know that with the passing of time, these powers must be conquered and forever ended.

We will now picture to ourselves that the path into the future and the path into the past each lead to the same point, a conception that present-day human beings find most difficult to grasp. Let us take as an example a circle; if we pass along the circumference from the lowest point in one direction, we come to the opposite point above; if, however, we continue along the other side, we come to the point at which we started. When we consider a larger circle, then the circumference is less curved, and we must traverse a greater distance in each case. We will now suppose that the circle expands ever more and more; ultimately, the path on either side becomes a straight line and is infinite. But just before the circle becomes infinite, we would reach the same point whether we went by the one path or the other. Why, then, should not the same happen when the circumference is so expanded that the periphery becomes a straight line? In this case the point at infinity on the one must be identical with that on the other, and therefore we must be able to travel to it from the lowest point in one sense (say, positive) and return as if coming from the opposite (negative) direction. This means that when our conception is infinite, we have a straight line extending without limit on either side but which is, in reality, the circumference of an infinite circle.

The abstraction given here lies at the basis of Zarathustra's conception of what he termed Zaruana Akarana. Here, with regard to time, we look in one direction into the future and in the other into the past; when we consider an infinite period, time closes in upon itself as in a circle. This self-contained and infinite time circle is symbolically represented as a serpent eternally biting its own tail, and into it is woven upon the one side "the Power of Light," shedding upon us continually a greater and greater radiance, and upon the other "the Power of Darkness," becoming ever more and more profound. When we are midway, then is the light (Ormuzd) intermingled with the shadows (Ahriman); all is interwoven in the self-embracing infinite flux of time Zaruana Akarana.

There is something more about this ancient cosmic conception: Its basic ideas were treated seriously; there were no mere vague statements such as this: "Without and remote from all that is material in this perceptual world, beyond those things that affect our eyes, our ears, and our sense organs in general, abides the Spirit." It was definitely asserted that in everything that could be seen and apprehended could be discerned something of the nature of spirit signs, or a manifestation of the spirit world.

If we take a sheet of paper upon which are inscribed alphabetical characters, we may combine the characters into words, but we must first have learned how to read. Without this ability, no one could read about Zarathustra, for they would merely perceive certain characters that could only be followed with the eyes. Actual reading can take place only after it is clearly understood how to connect such characters with that which is within the soul. Zarathustra discerned a written sign underlying all that was in the perceptual world, particularly in the manner in which the stars are grouped in the universe. Just as we recognize written characters upon paper, so did Zarathustra descry in the starry firmament something similar to letters, conveying a message from the spirit world. Hence arose an art of penetrating into the world of spirit, of deciphering the signs indicated by the arrangement of the stars, and of

finding a method of reading and construing from their movements and order in what manner and way those spiritual beings
that are without inscribe the facts concerning their activities in
space.

Zarathustra and his disciples had a paramount interest in
these matters. To them it was a most important sign that
Ahura Mazdao, in order to accomplish his creations and to
reveal his message to the world, should (in the language of
modern astronomy) "describe a circular path." This fact was
regarded as a sign traced in the heavens that indicated the manner in which Ahura Mazdao worked and the relation that his
activities bore to the universe as a whole. It is important that
Zarathustra was able to point out that the constellations of the
zodiac, taken together as forming a closed curve in space,
should symbolize a continuous and also retroactive time flux.
We can realize that there is indeed a most profound significance underlying the statement that one branch of this time
curve stretches outward into the future while the other leads
backward into the remote past. Zaruana Akarana is that bright
band of stars later known as the zodiac, that self-contained
timeline ever traversed by Ormuzd, the Spirit of Light. In
other words, the passage of the sun across the constellations of
the zodiac is an expression of the activity of Ormuzd, while
the zodiac itself is the symbol of Zaruana Akarana. In reality,
Zaruana Akarana and the zodiac are identical terms, in the
same way as are Ormuzd and Ahura Mazdao.

There are two special circumstances to be considered in this
connection. First, there is the passage of the sun through the
zodiac that takes place while it is light, as in the summer. At
such time the solar radiance falls full upon the earth, bringing
with it the power emanating from those spiritual forces ever

flowing outward from the light realms of Ormuzd. That part
of the zodiac traversed by Ahura Mazdao in the daytime, or
during the summer, denotes the manner in which he works and
weaves unhindered by Ahriman. On the other hand, those
zodiacal constellations that lie far beneath the horizon—dark
regions through which we might picture the passage of Angra
Mainyus—are symbolic of the kingdom of the shadows.

We have stated that Zarathustra regarded Ormuzd as associated with the bright sections of the zodiac (Zaruana Akarana),
while he looked upon Ahriman as connected with the gloom. In
what way do the activities of Ormuzd and Ahriman find expression in our material world? In order to understand this point, we
must realize that the effect of the solar rays is different in the
morning from that at noon, varying as the sun ascends from
Aries to Taurus and again during its descent toward the horizon.
The influence exerted is not the same in winter as in summer
and differs with every passing sign of the zodiac. Zarathustra
regarded the changing aspects of the sun in connection with the
zodiacal constellations as symbolic of the activities of Ormuzd
proceeding from different directions and from which came
those spiritual beings that are both his servants and his sons and
who are ready at all times to execute his commands. These are
the "Amschaspands" or "Ameschas Pentas," subservient entities
to each of whom is allotted some special duty.

While Ormuzd controls all active functions in the light
realms, the Amschaspands undertake that specific work which
finds expression in the transmission of the sun's light when it is
in Aries, Taurus, Cancer, and so on. But the true vital activity
of Ormuzd is manifested in the full radiance of the sun, shining throughout all bright signs of the zodiac from Aries to
Libra or Scorpio. Following the Zarathustran line of thought,

we might say: "It is as though the evil powers of Ahriman came
through the earth from those dark regions where abide his servants—his own Amschaspands—who are opposed to the good
genii standing by the side of Ormuzd." Zarathustra actually
distinguished twelve different subservient spirit entities—six
or seven on the side of Ormuzd and five or six on that of Ahriman. These are regarded as typical of good or evil genii
(Amaschas Pentas—lower spirits), according to whether their
influence comes with the sun's rays from the bright signs of the
zodiac or emanates from those that are in gloom.

Goethe had the subservient spirits of Ormuzd in mind when
he wrote the following words at the beginning of *Faust* in the
"Prologue of Heaven":

But ye, God's sons in love and duty,
Enjoy the rich, the ever-living Beauty
Creative Power, that works eternal schemes,
Clasp you in bonds of love, relaxing never,
And what in wavering apparition gleams
Fix in its place with thoughts that stand for ever![1]
(Trans: Bayard Taylor)

It is apparent in this passage that the conception which
Goethe formed of "God's sons" as the servants of the Highest
Divine Power is similar to Zarathustra's concept concerning

---

1. Doch ihr, die echten Göttersöhne,
   Erfreut euch der lebendig reichen Schöne!
   Das Werdende, das ewig wirkt und lebt,
   Umfass euch mit der Liebe holden Schranken,
   Und was in schwankender Erscheinung schwebt,
   Befestiget mit dauernden Gedanken.

the Amschaspands, of which he recognized, as noted, twelve different kinds. Again, subservient to these Amschaspand entities, according to Zarathustranism, are still lower orders of spiritual powers or forces, among which some twenty-eight separate types are usually distinguished. These are the so-called "Izarads" or "Izeds"; the number of different classes into which they may be divided is, however, indeterminate, being variously estimated from twenty-four to twenty-eight and even as high as thirty-one. There is yet a third division of spiritual powers or forces, termed by Zarathustra "Ferruhars" or "Frawaschars." According to our conceptions, the Ferruhars have the least influence of any upon our tendencies and dispositions in the material world and are regarded as that spiritual element which permeates the great macrocosm and underlies all perceptual physical activity. They are the reality behind everything of which we are conscious and appears to us as merely external and material.

While we picture the Amschaspands as controlling the twelve forces at work during all physical effects engendered by the action of light and the Izeds as governing those that influence the animal kingdom, so do we consider the Ferruhars, in addition to possessing the quality mentioned earlier, as spiritual entities having under their guidance the "group souls" of animals. Thus did Zarathustra discern a specialized realm beyond this perceptual universe—a perfectly organized superperceptual world—and his concept was absolutely definite and in no sense an abstraction. Behind Ormuzd and Ahriman, he pictured Zaruana Akarana, then the good and bad Amschaspands, below them the Izeds, and last the Ferruhars. The human being is a replica in miniature of the great universe, and therefore all forces operative in the cosmos must be present in some manner within each person's being. Just as the benevolent powers of Ormuzd are expressed during that inner struggle to attain to perfection and the unclean forces of Ahriman are in evidence when there is gloom and temptation, so do we find also the trace of other spiritual powers—those of the lower genii.

I will now make a definite statement, which when viewed from the standpoint of modern cosmic ideas is liable to awaken bitter feeling. I assert that before long it will be discovered and recognized by external science that a superperceptual element underlies all physical phenomena and that latent spirit exists in everything that comes within the limits of our sense perceptions. Further, science will be driven to admit that in the physical structure of human beings there is much that is a counterpart of those forces that permeate and spread life throughout the whole universe and which flow into the body, there to become condensed.

Let us go back to the Zarathustranism doctrine, which in many ways is similar to that of spiritual science. According to its concepts, Ormuzd and Ahriman are regarded as influencing humankind from without, Ormuzd being the source of inward impulses toward perfection while Ahriman is ever in opposition. The Amschaspands also exert spiritual activity; if we consider their forces as being, so to speak, condensed in the human being, then it should be possible to trace and recognize their action to the point of physical expression.

In Zarathustra's time, anatomy, as we understand it today, did not exist. Zarathustra and his disciples, by means of their spiritual insight, actually saw the cosmic streams to which reference has been made; they appeared to them in the form of twelve cosmic outpourings flooding in upon the human being, there to maintain activity. Thus it came about that the human head was regarded by Zarathustra's followers as a symbol of the inflowing of the seven good and five evil Amschaspands. Within the human being we have a continuance of the Amschaspand flux; how, then, is this flux to be recognized at this much later period? The anatomist has discovered that there are twelve principal pairs of brain nerves, which pass from the brain into the body. These are the physical counterparts, as it were, of the twelve condensed Amschaspand outflowings, namely, twelve pairs of nerves of extreme potency in bringing about either the highest perfection or the greatest evil. Here, then, we find reappearing in our present age, but transformed into material terms, that concept which had come to Zarathustra from the spirit world and which he preached to his disciples.

There is, however, in all this a point of controversy. It is so easy for anyone in our day to maintain that the statements of spiritual science become wholly fantastic when it is alleged that Zarathustra, speaking of twelve Amschaspands, had in mind something connected with the twelve pairs of nerves in the human head! But the time will come when the world will gain yet another item of knowledge, for it will be discovered in what manner and form the spirit, which permeates and lives throughout the universe, continues to be active in human beings. The old Zarathustranism has arisen once again in our modern physiology. For in the same way as the twenty-eight to thirty-one Izeds are the servants of the Amschaspands, so are the twenty-eight spinal nerves subordinate to those of the brain. Again, the Izeds, who are present in the outer universe as a spirit flux, enter the human body, and their sphere of action is in those nerves that stimulate the lower soul life of

[handwritten marginal note: human body similarities]

the human being; in these nerves they crystallize, as it were, and assume a condensed form. Where the Ized flux, as such, entirely ceases and the term "nerve" can no longer be applied is the actual center where our personality receives its crowning touch. Further, those of our thoughts that rise slightly above mere cognition and simple brain action are typical of the Ferruhars.

Our present period is connected in a remarkable manner with the doctrine of Zarathustra. Through his teachings and by means of his spiritual archetypes, Zarathustra was able to enlighten his people regarding those regions that spread beyond the perceptual world, while his imagery was ever a flowing contact with that which lies hidden behind the veil. With reference to this great doctrine, it is most significant that after it had acted as an inspiration to humanity for a long period, always tending to promote greater and greater effort in various directions of cultural progress—only to lose its influence from time to time—there should arise once more, in our day, a marked tendency toward a mystical current of thought.

It was the same with the Greeks after the two methods of approach to the spirit world had commingled, for they also at times showed a preference for either the mystical or the spiritual-scientific thought current. It is owing to the modern predominating interest in mysticism that many people find themselves drawn toward the Indian spiritual science or method of contemplation. Hence it is that the most essential and deeply significant aspects of Zarathustranism—in fact, its very essence—hardly appear in the spiritual life of our time, though there is abundant evidence of the nature of Zarathustra's concepts and his methods of thought. But all that lies at the very base and is absolutely vital to his doctrine is, in a sense, lost to our age. When once we realize that in Zarathustranism is contained the spiritual prototype of so many things that we have rediscovered in the domain of physical research (numerous examples of which might be quoted) and of others that will be rediscovered later, then will a fundamental chord in our culture give place to one that will be founded upon the old Zarathustran teachings. It is remarkable that the profound attention Zarathustranism paid to macrocosmic phenomena caused the world to recede, as it were, or appear of less moment, while in nearly all other beliefs with which a flood of mystical culture is associated the outer world plays an important part; this is also the case in our present-day materialism.

That great fundamental concept concerning two opposing basic qualities, which recurs again and again throughout the religious doctrines of the world, we regard in the following manner: We consider it as symbolized by the antithesis of the sexes—the male and the female—so that in the old religious systems founded upon mysticism, the gods and goddesses were in reality antithetical symbols of two opposing currents that flow throughout the universe. It is amazing that the teachings of Zarathustra should rise above these conceptions and picture the origin of spiritual activity in so different a manner, portraying the good as the resplendent and the evil as the shadows.

Hence the chaste beauty of Zarathustranism and its nobility, which transcends all those petty ideas that play so ugly a part in our time, when any endeavour is made to deepen the human being's conception of spiritual life. Where the Greek writers state that the Supreme Deity in order to create Ormuzd must also create Ahriman so that Ormuzd should obtain an antithesis, then in the opposition of Ahriman and Ormuzd we have an example of how one primordial force is conceived as set against another. This same idea finds expression in the Hebrew, where evil comes upon the world through the woman—Eve. But we find nothing in Zarathustranism concerning ills that the world suffered through the antithesis of the sexes.

All those hateful ideas that are disseminated throughout our daily literature, pervading our very thoughts and feelings and distorting the true significance of the phenomena of disease and health while failing to comprehend the intrinsic facts of life will disappear when that wholly different concept, the antithesis exhibited by Ormuzd and Ahriman—a conception so lofty and so powerful when compared with present-day paltry notions—is once more voiced in the words of Zarathustra and permeates and influences our modern culture. In this world all things pursue their appointed course, and nothing can hinder the ultimate triumph of Zarathustran conceptions, which will little by little insinuate themselves into the life of the people.

When we look upon Zarathustra in this way, we realize that he was indeed a spirit who in bygone times brought potent impulses to bear upon human culture. That such was the case becomes evident if we but follow the course of subsequent events that took place in Asia Minor and later among the people of Assyria and Babylonia on down to the Egyptian period and further even to the time of the spreading of Christianity. Everywhere we find in different lines of thought something that may be traced back and shown to have its origin in that Great Light that Zarathustra set blazing for humanity.

We can now understand how it was that a certain Greek writer (who wished to emphasize the fact that some among the leaders had always given their people instruction in matters that they would require only at a later period in their culture) should have stated that while Pythagoras had obtained all the knowledge that he could from the Egyptians concerning the methods of geometry, from the Phoenicians concerning arithmetic, and from the Chaldeans concerning astronomy—he was forced to turn to the successors of Zarathustra to learn the secret teachings regarding the relation of humanity to the spirit world and to obtain a true understanding of the proper conduct of life. The writer who made these statements regarding Pythagoras further asserts that the Zarathustranism method for the conduct of life leads us beyond antitheses and that all antitheses can be considered as culminating in the one great contrast of Good and Evil, which opposing condition can finally be absorbed only by the purging away of all evil, falsehood, and deceit. For instance, the worst enemy of Ormuzd is regarded as that one who bears the name of calumny, and calumny is one of the outstanding characteristics of Ahriman. The same writer states that Pythagoras failed to find the purest, the ideal ethical practice, namely, the one directed toward the moral purification of the human being, among the Egyptians, the Phoenicians, or the Chaldeans and that he had again to turn to Zarathustra's successors to acquire that lofty conception of the universe which leads humankind to the earnest belief that through self-purification alone may evil be overcome. Thus did the great nobility and oneness of Zarathustra's teachings become recognized among the ancients.

We would here mention that the statements made in this lecture are supported in every case by independent historical research, and we should carefully weigh all assertions coming from representatives of other sciences and judge for ourselves whether or not they are in accord with our fundamental concepts. For instance, take the case of Plutarch, when he said that in the sense of Zarathustranism, the essence of light as it affects the earth is regarded as of supreme loveliness and that its spiritual counterpart is truth. Here is a definite statement made by an ancient historian that is in complete agreement with all that has been said. We shall also find as we proceed that many historical events become clear and understandable when we take into consideration the various factors to which we have drawn attention.

Let us now go back to the ancient Vedantic conception; this was based upon the mystical merging of human beings within their very being, but before they can attain to the inner light of Brahma, they must meet with and pass through those passions and desires that are induced by wild, semihuman impulses within and which are opposed to that mystical withdrawal within the spirit-soul and into the eternal inner being. The Indians came to the conclusion that this could be accomplished only if, pending mystic merging in Brahma, they could successfully eliminate all that we experience in the perceptual world that stimulates sensuous desires and allures through colors and through sounds. So long as these sensations play a part during our meditations, so long do we keep within us an enemy opposed to our mystical attainment to perfection.

The Indian teacher said: "Put away from yourselves all that can enter the soul through the powers that are external; merge yourselves solely within your very being—descend to the Devas—and when you have vanquished the lower Devas, then will you find yourselves within the kingdom of the Deva of

Brahma. But shun the realm of the Asuras, whence come those malignant ones who would thrust themselves upon you from the outer world of Maya; from all such you must turn away, whatsoever may befall."

Zarathustra, on the other hand, spoke to his disciples after this fashion: "Those who follow the leaders among the people of the South can make no advance along the path they have chosen because of the different order of their search after those things that are of the Spirit; in such manner can no nation make headway. The call is not alone to mystic contemplation and to dreaming but to live in a world that provides freely of all that is needful— humanity's mission lies with the art of agriculture and the promotion of civilization. You must not regard all things as merely maya, but you must penetrate that veil of colors and of sounds that is spread around you and avoid everything that may be of the nature of the Devas and which because of your inner egoism would hold you in its grasp. The region wherein abide the lower Asuras must be traversed; through this you must force your way even up to the highest. But since your being has been especially organized and adapted to this intent, you must ever shun the dark realms of the Devas."

In India the teaching of the Rishis was otherwise, for they said to their followers: "Your beings are *not* suitably organized to seek that which lies within the Kingdom of the Asuras— therefore avoid this region and descend to that of the Devas." Such was the difference between the Indian and Persian culture. The Indian peoples were taught that they must shun the Asuras and regard them as evil spirits, because through the method of their culture they were aware only of the lower Asuras. On the other hand, the Persians, who found only low types of Devas in the Devas' regions, were adjured by their leaders thus: "Enter the kingdom of the Asuras, for you are so constituted that you may attain even unto the highest of them."

There lay within the impulse that Zarathustra gave to humankind a great fervor, which found expression when he said, "I have a gift to bestow upon humanity that shall endure and live throughout the ages and will smooth the upward path, overcoming all false doctrines, which are but obstacles diverting human beings from their struggle toward the attainment of perfection." Thus did Zarathustra feel himself to be the servant of Ahura Mazdao, and as such he experienced personally the opposition of Ahriman, over whose principles his teachings should enable humankind to achieve a sweeping victory. This conviction he expressed in impressive and beautiful words, to which reference is found in ancient documents. These, however, were necessarily inscribed at a later date, but what spiritual science tells us concerning Zarathustra and his pronouncements comes from other sources. Throughout all his telling adjurations there rings forth the inner impulse of his mission, and we feel the power of that great passion that overcame him, when as the opponent of Ahriman and the Principle of Darkness, he said, "I will speak! Draw nigh and listen unto me, ye that come with longing from afar, and ye from near at hand—mark my words!—No more shall he, the Evil One, this false teacher, conquer the Spirit of Good. Too long hath his vile breath bemingled human voice and human speech. But now I will denounce him in the words that the Highest—the First One—has put into my mouth, the words that Ahura Mazdao has spoken. To him who will not harken unto my words and who will not heed that which I say unto you—to him will come evil—and that ere ever the world hath ended its cycles."

Thus spoke Zarathustra, and we can but feel that he had
something to impart to humanity, which would leave its
impress throughout all later cultural periods. Those among us
who have understanding and will pay attention to that which
persists in our time—even if it is only dimly apparent—those
who will note with spiritual discernment the tenor of our culture can even yet, after thousands of years, recognize the echo
of the Zarathustran teachings. Hence it is that we number Zarathustra among great leaders such as Hermes, Buddha, Moses,
and others, about whom we shall have much to say in subsequent lectures. The spiritual gifts possessed by these great ones
and the position they occupied among human beings are indicated and fitly expressed in the following words:

God sends us Spirits that shine as stars,
From the spheres of eternal love.
May we behold that glorious light,
They reflect from the realms above.[2]

---

2. Es leuchten gleich Sternen
   Am Himmel des ewigen Seins
   Die gottgesandten Geister.
   Gelingen möge es alien Menschenseelen,
   Im Reiche des Erdenseins
   Zu schauen ihrer Flammen Licht!

2. HERMES

IT IS INDEED significant that a man of such outstanding intellect as Johannes Kepler should have been moved, at the very dawn of modern scientific development, to express the feelings that came over him while he was engaged in astronomical research in words somewhat as follows: "During my attempt to discover the manner of the passing of the planets around the sun, I have sought to peer into the deep secrets of the cosmos, the while it has often seemed as if my fancy had led me into the mysterious sanctuaries of the old Egyptians—to touch their most holy vessels and draw them forth that I might bestow them upon a new world. At such moments the thought has come to me that only in the future will the true purport and intent of my message be disclosed." It is of great importance to spiritual science to follow the gradual development of the human spirit from epoch to epoch as it slowly evolves and, pressing ever upward, emerges from the dark shadows of the past. Hence it is that the study of ancient Egyptian culture and spiritual life is of especial moment. This is found to be particularly the case when we endeavor to picture and live in the atmosphere and conditions associated with the latter. The echoes that reach us from the dim gray vistas of bygone times seem as full of mystery as is the countenance of the Sphinx itself, which stands so grimly as a monument to ancient Egyptian civilization. This mystery becomes intensified as modern external scientific research finds that it is constrained to delve ever deeper and deeper into the remote past in order to throw light upon later Egyptian culture, regarding which most important documents are extant. Such investigations have found traces of certain things clearly related to the active cultural life of Egypt that date back to a period at least seven thousand years before the beginning of the Christian era. Here, then, is one reason why this particular civilization is of such paramount interest. But there is another: Although they live in times of broader and more general enlightenment, present-day human beings nevertheless have a feeling, whether acceptable or not, that this ancient culture is in some singular and mysterious manner connected with their own aims and ideals.

Here we find one of the greatest scientists of modern times overcome by a sense of such close relation to the ancient Egyptian culture that he could find no better way of expressing the fundamental concepts underlying his work than by representing them as a regeneration, naturally differing as to word and form, of the occult doctrines taught to the disciples and followers in the bygone Egyptian sanctuaries. It is therefore a matter of the greatest interest to us that we should realize the actual sentiments of these olden Egyptian peoples in regard to the whole meaning and nature of their civilization.

There is an ancient legend that has been handed down through Greek tradition which is most suggestive not only of what the Egyptians themselves felt regarding their culture but also of the way in which their civilization was looked upon by the ancients as a whole. We are told that an Egyptian sage once said to Solon: "You Greeks are still children. You have never grown up, and all your knowledge has been acquired through your own human observation and senses. You have neither traditions nor doctrines gray with age." We first learn what is implied by the expression "doctrines gray with age" when the methods of spiritual science are employed in the effort to throw light upon the nature and significance of Egyptian thought and feeling. As has been stated earlier, when we approach this matter, we must bear in mind that during successive periods of their development human beings gradually acquired different forms of consciousness. The order of conscious apprehension that is ours today—with its scientific method of thought, through which we realize the outer world by virtue of our senses working in conjunction with reason and intellect—did not always exist. Deep down, underlying all human cognition, there is what we term *evolution*, and evolution affects not only the outer world of form but also the disposition of the human soul. It follows that we can really understand the events that took place at the ancient centers of culture only when we accept that knowledge which spiritual science can alone obtain, from the sources of information at its disposal. We thus learn that in olden times, instead of our present intellectual consciousness, there existed a clairvoyant state that differed from our customary normal conscious condition, of which we are aware from the moment we awake until we again fall asleep. On the other hand, the ancient clairvoyant state cannot be likened to the insensibility produced by slumber. Hence, the primeval consciousness of the prehistoric human being should be regarded as an intermediate condition now only faintly apparent and retained, one might say, atavistically in the form of an attenuated heritage in the picture world of our dreams.

Dreams are, for the most part, chaotic in character and therefore meaningless in their relation to ordinary life. But the old
clairvoyant consciousness, which also found expression in
imagery (though often of a somewhat subdued and visionary
nature), was nevertheless a truly clairvoyant gift, and its sym-
bolical manifestations had reference not to our physical world
but to that realm that lies beyond all material things—in other
words, the world of spirit. We can say that in reality all clairvoyant consciousness, including the dream state of the primitive human being as well as that acquired today through those
methods to which we have previously referred, finds expression
pictorially and not in concepts and ideas, as is the case with
externalized physical consciousness. It is for the possessor of
such a faculty to interpret the symbols presented in terms of
those spiritual realities that underlie all physical perceptual
phenomena.

We have now reached a point where we can look back on the
evolution of the ancient races and say for certain that those
wondrous visions of bygone times of which tradition tells us
were not born of childish fantasy and false conception of the
works of nature (this, as I have pointed out, is the widespread
opinion in materialistic circles of today) but were in truth pictures of the spirit world flashed before the souls of human
beings in that now long-distant past. One who seriously studies the old mythologies and legends not from the point of
view of modern materialistic thought but with an understanding of the creation and spiritual activities of humankind will

find in these strange stories a certain coherence that harmonizes wonderfully with those cosmic principles that dominate
all physical, chemical, and biological laws; there rings
throughout the ancient mythological and religious systems a

tone of spiritual reality from which they acquire a true significance.

We must clearly realize that the peoples of the various
nations, each according to disposition, temperament, and racial
or folk character, formed different conceptions of that vision
world in which they conceived higher powers to be actively
operating behind the accustomed forces of nature. Further,
during the gradual course of evolution, humankind passed
through many transitionary stages between that of the consciousness of the ancients and our present-day objective conscious state. As time went on, the power necessary to the old
clairvoyance dimmed, and the visions faded. One might say
that the doors leading to the higher realms were slowly closed,
so that the pictures manifested to those whose souls could still
peer into the spirit world held less and less spiritual force until,
toward the end, only the lowest stages of supersensible activity
could be apprehended. Finally, this primeval clairvoyant power
died out insofar as humanity in general was concerned, and
humanity's vision became limited to that which is of the material world and to the apprehension of physical concepts and
things. From that time on the study of the interrelation of
these factors led step by step to the birth of modern science.
Thus it came about that when the old clairvoyant state was
past, our present intellectual consciousness gradually developed in diverse ways among the different nations.

The mission of the Egyptian peoples was of a very special
nature. All that we know regarding ancient times, even that
knowledge attained through modern Egyptian research, if
rightly understood, tends to verify the statements of spiritual
science regarding the allotted task and true purpose of the
Egyptian race. It was ordained that these olden peoples should

still be imbued with a sufficiency of that primal power which would enable them to look back into the misty past when their leaders, by virtue of outstanding individualities and highly developed clairvoyant faculties, could gaze far into the mysteries of the spirit world. [Spiritual science asserts that it was in accordance with "The Great Eternal Plan" that the Egyptians should gain wisdom and understanding from this source, to be a guide and a benefit in the development of humankind.] And we have learned that it was to this end that this great nation was still permitted to retain a certain measure of that fast-fading clairvoyant power so closely associated with a specific disposition of soul. Although these qualities were at that time weak and waning in intensity, nevertheless they continued to be active until a comparatively late period in Egyptian history.

We can therefore make this statement: The Egyptians, until less than a thousand years before the Christian era, had actual experience of a mode of vision differing from that with which we are familiar in everyday life, when we merely open our eyes and make use of our intellect; they knew that through this gift humans were enabled to behold the spiritual realms. The later Egyptians, however, were unable to penetrate beyond the nethermost regions, as portrayed in their pictorial visions; nonetheless, they had power to recall those bygone times in the golden age of Egyptian culture when their priesthood could gaze both far and deeply into the world of spirit.

All knowledge obtained through visions was most carefully guarded and secretly preserved for thousands of years with the greatest piety, thankfulness, and religious feeling, especially by the older Egyptians. At a later period, those among the people who still retained some clairvoyant power expressed themselves in this fashion: "We can yet discern a lower spiritual realm—

we know therefore that it is possible for humankind to look upon a spirit world; to question this truth would be as sensible as to doubt that we can really see external objects with our eyes." Although these later Egyptians were able to apprehend only weak echoes, as it were, of the inferior spiritual levels, nevertheless they felt and divined that in olden times human beings could indeed penetrate far into the mystic depths of that realm which lies beyond all physical sense perceptions. There is a doctrine gray with age, still preserved in wonderful inscriptions in temples and upon columns. (It was this doctrine to which the sage referred when he spoke to Solon.) These inscriptions tell us of the broad and deep penetration of clairvoyant power in the remote past.

The being to whom the Egyptians attributed all the profundity of their primordial clairvoyant enlightenment they called the Great Wise One—the Old Hermes. When, at a later period, some other outstanding leader came to revive the ancient wisdom, he also called himself Hermes, according to an old custom prevalent among exalted Egyptian sages and because his followers believed that in him the primeval wisdom of the old Hermes lived once again. They named the first Hermes Trismegistos—the Thrice-Great Hermes. As a matter of fact, it was only the Greeks who used the name of Hermes, for among the Egyptians he was known as Thoth. In order to understand this being, it is necessary to realize what the Egyptians, under the influence of traditions concerning Thoth, regarded as true and characteristic cosmic mystics.

Such Egyptian beliefs as have come to us, one might say, from outside sources seem very strange indeed. Various gods of whom the most important ones are Osiris and Isis, are represented as not wholly human, often having a human body and an animal head or formed of the most varied combinations of humanlike and animal shapes. Remarkable religious legends have come down to us regarding this world of the gods. The veneration and worship of cats and other animals by this ancient race was most singular and went to such lengths that certain animals were considered holy and held in the greatest reverence; in them the Egyptians saw something akin to higher beings. It has been said that this veneration for animals was such that, for instance, when a cat that had lived for a long time in one house died, there was much weeping and lamentation. If an Egyptian observed a dead animal lying by the wayside, he did not dare to go near it for fear that someone might accuse him of having slain it, in which case he would be liable to severe punishment. Even during the time that Egypt was under Roman rule, so it has been said, any Roman who killed a cat went in danger of his life, because such an act produced an uproar among the Egyptians. This veneration of animals appears to us as a most enigmatic part of Egyptian thought and feeling.

Again, how extraordinary do the pyramids, with their quadrilateral bases and triangular sides, seem to modern humans and how mysterious are the sphinxes and all that modern research drags forth from the depths of this ancient civilization and brings to the surface to add to our knowledge an ever-increasing clarity. This question now arises: What place did all these strange ideas occupy in the image world of the souls of those olden peoples? What had they to say regarding those things that the Thrice-Great Hermes had taught them, and how did they come by these curious concepts?

We must henceforth accustom ourselves to seek in all legends a deeper meaning, especially in those that are the more important. It is to be assumed that the purpose of some of these legends is to convey to us in picture form information regarding certain laws that govern spiritual life and are set above external laws. As an example we have the fable of the god Osiris and the goddess Isis. It was Hermes himself who called the Egyptian legends "the Wise Counselors of Osiris." In all these fables Osiris is a being who in the gray dawn of primeval times lived in the region where human beings now dwell. In the legend Osiris—who is represented as a benefactor of humanity and under whose wise influence Hermes, or Thoth, gave to the Egyptians their ancient culture, even to the conduct of material life—was said to have an enemy whom the Greeks called Typhon. This enemy, Typhon, waylaid Osiris and slew him and then cut up his body, hid it in a coffin, and threw it into the sea. The goddess Isis, wife and sister of Osiris, sought her husband who had been thus torn from her by Typhon, or Seth. When she at last found him, she gathered together the pieces into which he had been divided and buried them here and there in various parts of the land; in these places temples were erected. Later, Isis gave birth to Horos. Horos was also a higher being, and his birth was brought about through spirit influence, which descended upon Isis from Osiris, who had meanwhile passed into another world. The mission of Horos was to vanquish Typhon and in a certain sense reestablish control of the life current emanating from Osiris, which would continue to flow and influence humankind.

A legend such as this must not be regarded simply as an allegory or as mere symbolism; in order to understand it rightly, we must enter into the whole world of Egyptian feeling and perception. It is far more important to do this than to form

abstract concepts and ideas, for by thus opening the mind we
can alone give life to the sentiments and thoughts associated
with the ideal forms of Osiris and Isis. Further, it is useless to
attempt to explain these two outstanding figures by saying that
Osiris represents the sun and Isis the moon and so forth—
thus giving them an astronomical interpretation, as is the custom of the sciences of today outside of spiritual science. Such a
theory leads to the belief that a legend of this nature is a mere
symbolic portrayal of certain events connected with the heavens, and this is not true. We must go far back to the primeval
feelings of the Egyptians and, using these as a starting point,
try to realize the whole peculiar nature of their uplifted vision
of the supersensible and conception of those invisible forces
beyond human apprehension that underlie the perceptual
world. It is the spiritual interrelation of these factors that finds
expression in the ideal forms of Osiris and Isis.

The old Egyptians associated these two figures with ideas
similar to the following: There is a latent higher spiritual
essence in all humankind that did not emanate from that material environment in which it now functions; at the beginning of
earthly life it entered into physical bodily existence in condensed form, there slowly to unfold and grow throughout the
ages. Our human state was preceded by another and more spiritual condition, and it is this primordial condition from which
the human being gradually developed. The Egyptian said:
"When I look into my soul, I realize that there is within me a
longing for spiritual things, a longing for that true spirituality
from which I have descended. I know that certain of the supersensible forces that operate in the region from which I come
still live within me and that the best of these forces are intimately related to the ultimate source of all superperceptual

activity. Thus do I feel within me an Osiris power, which placed me here—a spirit embodied in external human form. In times past, before I came to this state, I lived wholly in a spiritual realm, where my life was confused, dim, and instinctive in character. It was ordained that I be clothed with a material body so that I should experience and behold a physical world, in order that I might develop therein. I know truly that in the beginning I lived a life that, compared to this physical perceptual existence, was indeed of the spirit."

According to ancient Egyptian concepts, the primordial forces underlying human evolution were regarded as dual, the one element being termed Osiris while the other was known as Isis. Hence we have an Osiris-Isis duality. When we give ourselves over to inner contemplation and are moved by the feelings and perceptions of the old Egyptians concerning this dualism, we at once find that we are involved in a process of active and suggestive thought, leading to certain conclusions. In order to follow this mental process, we have only to consider the manner in which the mind operates when we think of some object, for instance, a triangle. In this case, active thought must precede the actual conception of the figure. After the soul has been thus engaged in primary contemplation, we then turn our minds passively to the result of our thought concepts and finally see the fruit of our mental activity pictured in the soul.

The act of thinking has the same relation to final thought as the act of conceiving to the final concept or activity to the result of activity or its ultimate product. If we contemplate our mental process when we picture the Egyptian past and are mindful of the mood of these ancient peoples, we realize that they looked upon the relation between Osiris and Isis in a manner somewhat similar to our conception of the order and outcome of thought activity. For instance, we might consider that activity should be regarded as a male or Father principle and that therefore the Osiris principle must be looked upon as an active male principle, a combative principle, that imbues the soul with thoughts and feelings of potency and vigor.

[We can form an idea of the old Egyptian concept concerning Osiris and Isis from the following considerations]: In the human physical body are certain components such as those that are active in the blood and those that are the basis of bone formation. The whole human system owes its being to the interaction of forces and matter, which combine to create and enter the material form; these elements can be physically recognized, but they were at one time dispersed and spread throughout the universe. A similar idea prevailed among the ancient Egyptians concerning their conception of the Osiris force, which was conceived as actively pervading the entire cosmos, as Osiris. Even as the elements that form the physical body enter into it, there to combine and become operative, so did those olden peoples picture the Osiris force as descending upon human beings to flow into their being and inspire within the power of constructive thought and cognition—the veritable Osiris force. On the other hand, the expression "Isis force" was applied to the universal, living cosmic influence that flows directly into the thoughts, concepts, and ideas of humankind. In this manner we must picture the uplifted vision in the souls of the old Egyptians, and it was thus that they regarded Osiris and Isis.

In the creation that surrounds us during our material exist- ence, the ancient consciousness could find no words with which to express concepts such as these, for everything about

us appeals alone to the senses and has meaning and value only
in a perceptual world, proffering no outer sign suggestive of a
superphysical region. Thus, in order to obtain something in
the nature of a written language, which could express all such
thoughts as moved the soul strongly—as for instance, when
the human being exclaimed, "The Osiris-Isis force works
within me"—the ancients reached out to the script written in
the firmament by the heavenly bodies. They said, "The supersensible power that the human being feels as Osiris can be
apprehended and expressed in perceptual terms if regarded as
that active force emanating from the sun and spread abroad in
the great cosmos. The Isis force may be pictured as the sun's
rays reflected from the moon, which waits upon the sun so
that she may pass on the power of his radiance in the form of
Isis influence. But until she receives his light, the moon is
dark—dark as a soul untouched by active uplifting thought."
When the old Egyptian said: "The sun and the moon that are
without reveal to me how I can best express, figuratively, my
ideas concerning all that I feel within my soul," he knew that
there was some hidden bond, in no way fortuitous, between
these two heavenly bodies that appear so full of mystery in the
vast universe—the light-giving sun and the dark moon every
ready to reflect his splendor. He realized as well that the light
dispersed in space and, when reflected, must bear some
unknown but definite relation to those supersensible powers of
which he was conscious.

When we look at a clock, we cannot see what it is that moves
the hands so mysteriously, apparently with the aid of little
demons, for all that can be seen is a mechanism. But we know
that underlying the whole mechanical structure is the thought
of the original designer, which had its origin in the *soul* of a

human being. In reality, the mechanism owes its construction
to something spiritual. Just as the movements of the hands of
a clock are mutually related and fundamentally dependent
upon certain mechanical laws of the universe and finally upon
those that are operative in the human soul (as when one
speaks of experiencing the influence of the Osiris-Isis force),
so are the movements of the sun and moon interrelated, and
these bodies appear to us as indicators on the face of a
mighty cosmic clock. The Egyptian did not merely say, "The
sun and moon are to me a perceptual symbol of the relation
between Osiris and Isis." Indeed, he felt and expressed himself thus: "That force which gives me life and is within underlies the mysterious bond existing between the sun and moon,
and it likewise endowed them with power to send forth light."

In the same way as Osiris and Isis were regarded with reference to the sun and moon, so were other heavenly bodies
looked upon as related to different gods. The ancient Egyptians considered that the positions of the various orbs in space
were not symbolic merely of their own supersensible experiences but likewise of those that tradition told them had been
the experiences of seers belonging to the remote past. Further,
they saw in the cosmic clock an expression of the activity of
those forces, the workings of which they felt in the ultimate
depths of the human soul. Thus it came about that this mighty
clock, this grand creation of moving orbs so wondrously interrelated with others that are fixed, was to the Egyptians a revelation of those mysterious spiritual powers that bring about the
ever-changing positions of the heavenly bodies and thus create
a universal script that humankind must learn to know and recognize as a means whereby superperceptual power is given perceptual expression.

Such were the feelings and perceptions that had been handed down to the old Egyptians from their ancient seers regarding a higher spiritual world of the existence of which they were wholly convinced, for they still retained a last remnant of primeval clairvoyant power. These olden peoples said, "We human beings had our true origin in an exalted spiritual realm, but we are now descended into a perceptual world in which manifest material things and physical happenings; nevertheless, we are indeed come from the world of Osiris and of Isis. All that is best and which strives within us and is fitted to attain to yet higher states of perfection has flowed in upon us from Osiris and from Isis and lives unseen within as active force. The physical human being was born of those conditions that are of the external perceptual world, and his material form is but a garment clothing the Osiris-Isis spirit within."

Predominant in the souls of the old Egyptians was a profound sentiment concerning primeval wisdom, which filled their whole soul life. The soul may indeed incline toward abstract notions, particularly the mathematical concepts of natural science, without in any way touching the moral and ethical factors of its life or affecting its fate or state of bliss. For instance, there may be discussion and debate relative to electrical and other forces without the soul's being moved to enter upon grave questions concerning humanity's ultimate destiny. On the other hand, we cannot ponder feelings and sentiments such as we have described regarding the spirit world and the inner relation of the soul's character to Osiris and Isis without arousing thoughts involving humankind's happiness, future, and moral impulses. When the mind is thus occupied, our meditations are prone to take this form: "There dwells in me a better self, but because of what I am within my physical

body, this 'better self' is repressed and draws back; it is therefore not at first apparent. An Osiris and an Isis nature are
fundamental to me; these, however, belong to a primordial
world, to a bygone golden age, to the holy past. Now they are
overcome by those forces that have fashioned the human form.
But the Osiris-Isis power has entered and persists within that
mortal covering that is ever subject to destruction through the
external forces of nature."

The legend of Osiris and Isis may be expressed in terms of
feeling and sentiment in the following manner: Osiris, the
higher power in human beings, which is spread throughout
cosmic space, is overcome by those forces that bring about
utter degeneration in all human nature. Typhon confined the
Osiris force within the body, as in a coffin formed to receive
the human being's spiritual counterpart; there the Osiris element lies concealed, invisible and unheeded by the outer world.
(The name Typhon has a linguistic connection to the words
Auflösen, meaning "to dissolve," and *Verwesen,* meaning "to
decompose.") The Isis nature, hidden within the confines of
the soul, was always mysterious to the Egyptians. They
thought that at some future period its influence would bring
humankind back to that state which they enjoyed in the beginning and that this return would ultimately be brought about
through the penetrative force of intellectual power. They fully
recognized that in humanity there is a latent disposition that
always strives to reendow Osiris with life.

The Isis force lies deep within the soul, and its profound
purpose is to lead human beings step by step away from their
present material state and bring them back once more to
Osiris. So long as human beings do not cling to the physical, it
is this Isis force that makes it possible for them (even though

they remain outwardly physical in a material world) to detach themselves from their perceptual nature and henceforth and for ever more look upward from within their being to that more exalted Ego which, in the opinion of the most advanced thinkers, lies so mysteriously veiled at the very root of human powers of thought and action. This being—not the outer physical one but the true inner human being, who has ever the stimulus to strive toward higher spiritual enlightenment—is, as it were, the earthborn son of that Osiris who did not go forth into the material world but remained as if concealed in the realms of the spirit. In their souls the Egyptians regarded this invisible personality that struggles toward the attainment of a higher self as Horos—the posthumous son of Osiris. It was thus that these old Egyptians visualized, with a certain feeling of sadness, the Osiris origin of the human. At the same time, they looked inward and said, "The soul has still retained something of the Isis force that gave birth to Horos, the possessor of that never-ceasing impulse to strive upward toward spiritual heights, and it is in that sublimity that the human being will once again find Osiris.

It is possible for present-day humanity to bring about this mystic meeting in two ways. The Egyptian said, "I have come from Osiris, and to Osiris I shall return. Because of my spiritual origin, Horos lies deep within my being, and Horos leads me on, back to Osiris—to his Father—who may alone be found in the world of spirit. For he can in no way enter into human being's physical nature; there he is overcome by the powers of Typhon, the external forces that underlie all destruction and decay." There are but two paths by which Osiris may be attained: The one is by way of the Portal of Death. The other passes not through the Gateway of Physical Dissolution, for Osiris may be reached through initiation and the consecration of life to sacred service.

Under the title *Christianity as Mystical Fact*,[3] I have gone more fully into this belief. The Egyptian conception was as follows: When human beings have passed through the Portal of Death and after certain necessary preparatory stages have been completed, they come to Osiris. Being freed from the earthly envelope, there awakes in them a consciousness of actual relationship with that supreme deity; they realize that henceforth they will be greeted as Osiris, for this form of salutation is always bestowed upon those who have experienced death and entered into the world of spirit.

The other pathway that likewise leads back to Osiris, that is, into the spiritual realms, is by way of initiation and holy devotion. Such was regarded by the Egyptians as a method through which knowledge might be gained of all that is supersensible and lies concealed in human nature—in other words of Isis, or the Isis power. We cannot penetrate into the depths of the soul and thus reach the Isis force within by virtue of mere earthly wisdom born of the experiences of daily life. Nevertheless, we have the means at hand whereby we may break through to this inner power and descend to the true Ego, there to find that this same Ego is ever enshrouded by all that is material in the human physical disposition. If, indeed, we can pierce this dark veil, then do we find ourselves at last in the Ego's spiritual home.

Thus it was that the old Egyptians said, "You will descend into your own inner being, but first comes your physical quality,

---

3. *Chrisitanity as Mystical Fact and the Mysteries of Antiquity*, (CW 8) SteinerBooks, 2006.

with all that it may express of that self that is yours. Through
this human disposition must you force a way. When you regard
the stones and the justness of the way they are made, when you
consider the plants and their inner life and the wonder of their
form, and when you look upon the animals about you—there,
in these three kingdoms of nature, you behold the outer world
as engendered of spiritual and supersensible powers. But when
you stand before a human being, look not alone upon the outer
form but seek that which is within, where abides the soul's
strength—even as the Isis force." In connection with the rites of
initiation, there were included certain instructions as to what
things should be observed during such time as the soul might
remain incarnated.

The experiences of all who have descended into their innermost being have been fundamentally the same as those that
come about at the time of passing, differing only in the manner of their occurrence. [One might say that if this method of
approaching the spirit realms were followed, then] *human beings*
must pass through the Portal of Death while they yet live. They must
learn to know the change from the physical to the superphysical outlook, from the material to the spiritual world—in other
words, they must acquire knowledge of the metamorphosis
that takes place at the time of actual death. In order that they
may obtain such enlightenment, those who would become initiated must take the way that leads them into the very depths
of their being, for in this way alone may true understanding
and experience be attained. When this method is employed,
the first real inner experience is connected with the blood, as
formed by nature. The blood is the physical agent of the Ego,
just as the nervous system forms the material medium in connection with [the three ultimate modes of consciousness,]

feeling, willing, and thinking. We have already referred to this matter in a previous lecture.

According to the ancient Egyptians, those who desire to descend into their being in order to realize a profound association with the primary material media must first pass down into the physical etheric sheath and enter the etheric confines of the soul. They must learn to become independent of that force in the blood upon which they normally rely. They can then give themselves up to the workings and the wonder of the blood's action. It is essential that humans first thoroughly understand their higher nature with respect to its physical aspect. To do so, they must learn to view the material being as a detached and wholly separate object. Now the human being can recognize and be fully conscious of an object, as a specific thing, only when external to it. Thus, they must learn to bring about this relation with respect to the self, if they would indeed comprehend the actuality of their being. It was for this reason that initiation was directed toward the development of such powers as enabled the soul forces to undergo certain experiences independently of physical media or agents, so that finally the aspirant could look down upon such media objectively, in the same way as the human spiritual element looks down upon the material body after death.

The primary duty of those who would know the Isis Mysteries was to acquire knowledge concerning their own blood, after which they underwent an experience that can be best described as "Drawing nigh unto the Threshold of Death." This was the first step in the Isis initiation, and those who would take it must have the power to regard their blood and being externally and to pass into that sheath which is the medium of the Isis nature. Further, neophytes were led before two doors within some holy sanctuary, the one closed and the other open. As they stood in that place, there came before them visions depicting the most intimate experiences of their lives, and they heard a voice saying, "It is thus that thou art; so dost thou appear when thou beholdest thy true self pictured in the soul." How remarkable are these teachings, the echoes of which are still heard after thousands of years have passed, and how wonderfully they harmonize with the human being's present-day beliefs, even though they have since received materialistic interpretation.

According to the ancient Egyptian seer, when human beings take the initial step and come upon the world of their inner form, they are there confronted by two doors: "Through two doors shalt thou enter, thy blood and thy innermost being." The anatomist would say, "Through two inlets situated in the valves on either side of the heart." [There are two pairs of valves in the heart, one on one side and one on the other; in each case, when one of these valves is open in order to let the blood flow into a part of the system, the adjacent one is closed.] They who want to penetrate beneath the outer form must pass through the open door, for the gateway that is closed merely confines the blood to its proper course. We thus find that the results of anatomical investigation are certainly analogous to those born of clairvoyant vision in olden times; although they are not so clear and accurate as are the conclusions of the modern anatomist, nevertheless they portray what the clairvoyant consciousness actually apprehended when it regarded the human being's inner form from an external standpoint.

The next step in the Isis initiation was what one might call the proving, or profound study of fire, air, and water. During this period initiates gained complete knowledge of the sheath quality of their Isis being, of the properties of fire and how it flows in the blood, using it as a medium, and becomes fluid. They also received instruction about how oxygen infiltrates into the system from the air. All this wisdom descended upon them—the understanding of fire, air, and water; the warmth of breath; and the true nature of the fluidity of the blood.

Thus it came about that aspirants, by virtue of the knowledge they acquired of their sheath quality through their newly born comprehension of the elements of fire, air, and water, became so purified that when their vision at last penetrated beneath the enfolding envelope, they entered into their own Isis nature. We might say that it was at this point that initiates felt for the first time they were in contact with their actual being, that they were able to realize they were indeed spiritual entities—no longer limited by their external relation to humanity—and that they truly beheld the wonder of the spiritual realms.

It is a definite law that we can look upon the sun only in the daytime, for at night it lies concealed by matter. But the powers in the spiritual world are never thus veiled to those who have acquired the true gift of sight, for they are best discerned when the physical eyes are closed to all material things. Symbolically, in the sense of the Isis initiation, we would say, "That person who is purified and initiated into the Isis Mysteries may discern that spiritual life and power to which the sun owes its origin, even though there be darkness as at midnight, for metaphorically speaking such a person may at all times behold the great orb of day and come face to face with the spirit beings of the superperceptual world."

Such was the description of the method or, one might say, the path leading to the Isis forces within. We are told that it could be traversed by all who during earthly life would but earnestly seek the deepest forces of the soul. There were, however, yet higher mysteries—the Mysteries of Osiris, in which it was made clear that through the medium of the Isis forces and by virtue of those supersensible primordial spiritual powers to which human beings owe their origin, they could exalt themselves even further and thus attain to Osiris. In other words, they were initiated into those methods by which the human soul might be so uplifted as to at last enter upon the presence of that supreme deity.

When the Egyptians wished to portray the nature and character of the relation between Isis and Osiris, they had recourse to the special script that is written in the firmament by the passage of the sun and moon, while in the case of other spiritual powers, reference was made to the movements and interrelations existing between the various stars.

Most prominent among the astronomical groups in such portrayals was the zodiac, with its condition of comparative immobility, and the planets that move across its constellations. It was in the revelations of the heavens, as manifested in spiritual symbols, that the old Egyptians found the true method of expressing those deep feelings that touched their souls. They knew that no earthly means were competent to indicate clearly the vital purpose of that urgent call to seek the Isis forces, that humankind might, through their aid, draw nearer to Osiris. These old Egyptians felt that in order to describe this purpose fittingly, they must reach out and make use of those bright groups of stars that ever shine in the firmament.

Hence it would appear that, in the beginning, written characters were brought down to the earth from the vault of heaven. We must thus regard Hermes—the Great Wise One—who, according to Egyptian tradition, lived upon the earth in the dawn of antiquity and was endowed with the most profound clairvoyant insight concerning the human being's relation to the Universe, as having possessed to a high degree the power of apprehending and explaining the true nature of the connection between the constellations and the forces of the spirit world and of interpreting the signs portraying events and happenings as expressed in the language of the stars, in terms of their mysterious interrelations. Now if in those olden days it was desired to enlighten the people with regard to the nature of the bond existing between Osiris and Isis, this matter was put forward in the form of an exoteric legend, but in the case of the initiates the subject was treated more explicitly by means of symbolic reference to the light that emanates from the sun and is reflected by the moon and the remarkable conditions governing its changes during the varying phases of the latter. In these phenomena the Egyptians found a practical and genuine analogy, expressive of the sacred link between the Isis force within the human soul and that supreme spiritual figure—Osiris.

From the movements of the heavenly bodies and the nature of their interrelations, there originated what we must regard as the very earliest form of written characters. Little as this fact is yet recognized, we would nevertheless draw attention to the following statement: If we consider the consonants of the alphabet, we note that they imitate the signs of the zodiac in their comparative repose, while the vowels and consonants are connected in a way that may be likened to the relationship that the planets and the forces which move them bear to the constellations of the zodiac as a whole.

The sentiments that moved the ancient Egyptians when their thoughts turned to Hermes were such as we have described, and they realized that his great illumination came from those spiritual powers that called to him out of the heavens, prompting him with counsel concerning that activity which persisted in the souls of humankind. And more than that, he was instructed even in the deeds of everyday life and in those directions in which such sciences as geometry and surveying were needed. Both of these Pythagoras learned from the Egyptians, who ascribed all this knowledge to the primordial wisdom of Hermes. One might say that the 'Old Wise One' saw in the interrelation of all things spread abroad upon the earth a counterpart of that which exists in the firmament and finds expression in the mystic writings of the stars. It was the Thrice-Blessed Hermes who first gave this stellar script to the world and through its aid and in the dawn of Egyptian life instilled into the minds of the people the elements of the science of mathematics, while he adjured them to look up to the heavens, there to seek guidance even regarding mundane matters.

The very life of the Egyptian nation in that olden time was dependent upon the overflowing of the Nile and the deposits that it swept down from the mountainous country to the south. We can therefore readily understand how absolutely essential it was that there should be a certain preknowledge of the date of the coming of flood periods, so that they might anticipate the accompanying changes in natural conditions thus brought about in the course of any particular year. In those early days the Egyptians still reckoned time according to the stellar script that was written in the canopy of heaven.

When Sirius, the Dog Star, was visible in the sign of Cancer, they knew that the sun would shortly enter that part of the zodiac from whence its rays would shine down upon the earth and conjure forth, as if by magic, the life brought to the earth by the deposits of the overflowing Nile. For this reason, they looked upon Sirius as "the Watcher," who gave them warning of what they might expect, and the movements of Sirius formed part of their celestial clock. They gazed upward with thankful hearts, for the timely warnings of their Watcher enabled them to cultivate and tend their land in such a way that it might best bring forth all things necessary to external life.

When such questions of import as these arose, these old Egyptian peoples sought enlightenment and guidance from those writings that they saw spread across the firmament. At the same time they looked back into that dim gray past when first they had learned that the passage of the stars was in truth an expression of movements among the parts of some mighty cosmic clock." In Thoth, or Hermes, they recognized that great spirit who, according to their ancient traditions, set down the very earliest chronicles concerning cosmic wisdom. From the inspiration that came to him through the wondrous stellar script, Hermes conceived the forms underlying the physical alphabet and, through their aid, taught humankind the principles of agriculture, geometry, and surveying; indeed, he instructed them in all things needful for the conduct of physical life. Physical life is nothing but the embodiment of that spiritual life so deeply interwoven throughout the cosmos, and it was from the cosmos that the spirit of wisdom descended upon Hermes. It was evident to the Egyptians of that period to which we refer that the influence of the Great

Wise One was still active throughout their civilization, and they felt that this mystic bond was both profound and intimate in character.

The method adopted by the old Egyptians for the purpose of time calculations and which continued in use for many centuries was convenient in operation and lent itself readily to all simple computations of this nature. They regarded the year as made up of *exactly* 365 days, which they divided into twelve months each having 30 days, leaving five days over, which were accounted for separately. But modern astronomy tells us that if this method were to be employed, one quarter day every year is not taken into account. [The actual difference is 6 hours, 9 minutes, and 9 seconds.] Therefore, the Egyptian year came to an end one quarter day too soon. This difference gradually spread backward through the months until a coincidence was reached at the beginning of a certain year; such coincidence took place every 4 × 365 years. Thus, after the lapse of 1,460 years, the terrestrial time estimate would be for a moment in agreement with astronomical conditions, because at that particular moment the sum of the annual differences would be equivalent to one whole year.

Let us now suppose that at a certain time in 1322 B.C.E. an Egyptian looked up into the heavens. There, at that moment, any visible constellation would occupy a definite position in the firmament [which position could be used as a basis of computation]. If we calculate backward over a period of 3 × 1,460 years from 1322 B.C.E., we come to the year 5702 B.C.E.; it was at some time prior to this date to which the Egyptians ascribed the dawn of that primordial Holy Wisdom which came to them in the beginning. They said, "In bygone times human beings' power of clairvoyance was truly at its highest, but with the passing of each great Sun Period [of 1,460 years, which brought about the balance of terrestrial reckoning] the divine gift of "clear seeing" gradually faded, until in this fourth stage in which we now live it is weak and ever failing. Our civilization reaches far into the remoteness of antiquity, where the voice of tradition is all but stilled. In thought we hark back beyond three long cosmic periods to that glorious and distant past when our greatest teacher, his disciples, and his successors imparted to us the elements of the ancient wisdom that now finds expression—albeit in strangely altered form—in the character of our script; our mathematics, geometry, surveying; our general conduct of life; and also in our study of the heavens. We regard the cosmic adjustment of our human computation, with its convenient factors of 12 × 30 days and five supplementary, as a sign that we are ever subject to correction by the divine powers of the spirit world, because through error of thought and reason we have turned away from Osiris and from Isis. We cannot with exactitude measure the year's length, but when our eyes are raised on high, we can gaze into that hidden world from whence those spirit powers ever guide the courses of the stars, remedy our faults, and bring harmony where the human being has failed to find the truth."

From this it is clear that the old Egyptians realized the feebleness of human beings' powers of intellect and understanding, so that even in the case of their chronology they sought the aid of those higher spiritual forces and beings beyond the veil—beings who correct, watch over, and protect humankind during the activities and experiences of earth life, bringing to bear upon these problems the mystic laws of the great cosmos. Hermes, or Thoth, was held in greatest veneration as one inspired by the ever-vigilant heavenly powers, and in the souls of these ancient peoples this outstanding personality was looked upon not merely as a great teacher but as a being who was indeed exalted and whom they regarded with the most profound feelings of reverence and thankfulness, so that they cried out: "All that we have comes from Thee. Thou went on High in the dim gray dawn of antiquity and Thou hast sent down, by those who were the carriers of Thy traditions, all that flows throughout external civilization and which is of greatest human service." With reference to the actual creator of all supersensible forces and those who watch over them as well as Osiris and Hermes, or Thoth, the Egyptians not only felt in their souls that they were imbued with knowledge begotten of wisdom but indeed experienced a sentiment in the deepest moral sense of greatest veneration and gratitude.

The graphic descriptions of the past tell us that the wisdom of the ancient Egyptians was permeated throughout with a certain religious quality and mood, particularly noticeable in olden times, but by degrees these characteristics became less and less marked. In those days the people felt all knowledge to be closely associated with holiness, all wisdom with piety, and all science with religion. As this attitude waned, it gradually decreased in purity of form and expression. A similar change has taken place throughout the evolution of humankind among all those various civilizations whose mission has been to alter the trend of spiritual thought and lead it in some wholly new direction. When each nation had reached the pinnacle of achievement and its task was ended, there followed a period of decadence.

The greater part of our knowledge concerning ancient Egyptian culture is connected with an epoch of this nature, and the significance of all that lies beyond is merely a matter of conjecture and supposition. For instance, what is the true meaning of that extraordinary and to us grotesque worship of animals in that bygone age and of the curious feeling of awe we experience when our thoughts dwell upon the pyramids? The Egyptians themselves tell us that there was an era during which not only humankind but also beings from the higher spiritual realms descended upon the earth. This was in the beginning, before the knowledge and wisdom that was then granted had truly developed and become active.

aliens?

If we would indeed know the innermost nature of human beings, we must not alone regard the outer form but penetrate to the true self within. All external qualities with which we come in contact are but stages of manifestation that have remained in situ, one might say, and are seen as if representing in powerful, albeit diminutive imagery ancient principles dominant in the three kingdoms of nature. Consider the world of minerals and of rocks—here we find those same relations of form that human beings used in the architecture of the pyramids. The inner forces of plant life are expressed in the beauty of the lotus flower. And distributed along the path that culminates in the human being, we find in brute creation existences that have not attained to the higher level of humanity; they are a sort of crystallization of divine forces that have been embodied and scattered abroad in separate and distinct animal shapes.

We can well imagine that the feelings of the old Egyptians gave rise to thoughts of this nature when they recognized in animal life a manifestation of the unaltered primordial forces of the gods. For they looked back into the gray past, when all earthly things were begotten of divine supersensible powers and developed under their guidance. From this concept the

Egyptians conjectured that among the creations in nature's three kingdoms certain of these higher primal forces, which had lived on unchanged over a long period, had ultimately undergone some intimate modification that had raised them to that higher standard exhibited in the human form. When considering these ancient peoples, we must ever have regard for their feelings and perceptions and the necessities of their life. It is from these factors that we can best realize how close was the moral bond between their wisdom and the soul, so that the latter might not swerve from the path of rectitude and morality. The Egyptians believed that because of the manner in which the spirit world was created and fashioned by the divine supersensible powers there must be some definite moral relation that extends to the creatures of the animal kingdom. The grotesque and singular modes in which this concept ultimately found expression came about only after the final decline of the nation had commenced.

From the study of the later periods of Egyptian culture it is clear that human frailty and imperfection were unknown in primordial times, for we learn from this source that in the early dawn of Egyptian life civilization was of a high standard, and it was then that humans knew and experienced the most intimate divine spiritual revelations. We must not fall into that error, so common in our days, of assuming that all forms of human culture had their inception under the most simple and primitive conditions. In reality, it was only after the impulse imparted by those first glorious blessings had waned and a period of decline had set in that human life became crude and uncultured. For this reason we should not look upon the barbaric tribes merely as peoples in whom intellect is expressed in its most elementary form; on the contrary, we must consider the aboriginal races as representative of civilizations that have fallen away from some exalted primordial state. This assertion is not at all to the liking of that branch of science which would have us believe that all culture had its inception under the most elementary conditions, such as those still found among the savages of our time. Nevertheless, spiritual science affirms, by virtue of knowledge obtained through the medium of its special methods, that the primitive states of humankind are in truth manifestations of long-perished civilizations and that all human life had its inception under cultural conditions directly inspired by divine beings—mentors from the spirit world—who descended to the earth in the dim dawn of antiquity and over whose deeds is cast a veil impenetrable to external history.

Human beings have long believed that if we trace life's course backward through the ages we should in the end arrive at childish conditions, similar to those found among barbaric peoples. It was certainly not expected that in so doing we would find ourselves confronted with noble and exalted concepts and theories. Spiritual science definitely asserts that if we peer into the past, at the beginning of human life we shall not find rudimentary cultural states but instead lofty and glorious civilizations, which at some later period fell away from their first high spiritual standard. At this point we might well ask, "Does this assertion, as advanced by spiritual science, bring it into conflict with the results of modern scientific research—the logical methods of which delve deeply and without prejudice into all matters that come within the scope of its investigations?" Let us see how external science itself replies to this question.

With this object I will give a literal quotation from a recent work by Alfred Jeremias [Licentiate Doctor and Lecturer at the University of Leipzig], entitled *The Old Testament in the Light of the*

Ancient East.[4] From the text we learn that external science, while engaged in the gradual unfoldment of ancient history, has reached back into the remote past and there found traces of a highly spiritual primeval civilization, whose culture was imbued with the most momentous and intellectual conceptions. It is further emphasized that those cultural states, which we are so accustomed to term barbaric, should in reality be regarded as typical of primordial civilizations that have fallen away from some higher level. The actual quotation to which I have referred is as follows:

> The earliest records, as well as the whole ancient civilized life about the Euphrates valley, indicate the existence of a scientific and at the same time religious theoretical conception that was not confined merely to the occult doctrines of the temple; in accordance with its precepts, state organizations were regulated and conducted, justice declared, and property administered and protected. The more ancient the period to which we can look back, the

---

4. *The Old Testament in the Light of the Ancient East, (Der Einfluss Babyloniens auf das Verstiindnis des Alten Testamentes)*, Alfred Jeremias. 2 vols. Translated from the second German edition by C. L. Beaumont and edited by the Reverend Canon C. H. W. Johns, Litt.D. Published by Williams and Morgate, 1911.

"Die ältesten Urkunden sowie das gesamte euphratensische Kulturleben setzen eine wissenschaftliche und zugleich religiöse Theorie voraus, die nicht etwa nur in den Geheimlehren der Tempel ihr Dasein fristet, sondern nach der die staatlichen Organisationen geregelt sind, nach der Recht gesprochen, das Eigentum verwaltet und geschützt wird. Je höher das Altertum ist, in das wir blickenkönnen, um so Ausschliesslicher herrscht die Theorie; erst mit dem Verfall der alten euphratensischen Kultur kommen andere Mächte zur Geltung."

more absolute does the control exercised by this concept appear. It was only after the downfall of the primal Euphratean civilization that the influence of other powers began to make itself felt.

Thus do we honor and revere Hermes, even as we venerate the great Zarathustra. To us he shines forth as one of those grand outstanding individualities—veritable leaders of humankind—the very thought of whom engenders a feeling of enhanced power within and begets the certain conviction through which we know that the spirit is not merely abroad in the world but in fact weaves beneath all earthly deeds and is ever active throughout the evolution of humanity. Then are our lives strengthened, a fuller confidence is in our every action, hopes are assured, and destiny stands out the more clearly before us. It is at such times that we exclaim, "Those yet to be born will surely lift up their hearts to the glorious spirit mentors who were in the beginning and will seek the truth of their being in the gifts that are of the inner forces of the soul. They shall acknowledge and discern in the ever-recurrent impulses that come as an upward urge to humankind the workings of a divine power and the eternal manifestations of those Great Ones from the spirit world." From this excerpt it is clear that external science has truly made a beginning toward the opening up of new paths that tend to bring harmony and agreement into those matters [so often regarded as controversial] that it is the province of spiritual science to bring forward and impress upon our present civilization. In a previous lecture we have drawn attention to a similar progress in connection with the science of geology. If in the future we continue to advance in like fashion, we shall gradually be compelled to recede further and further from that dull and lifeless conception that would have us regard all primordial civilization as primitive and childish in its nature. Then, indeed, shall we be led back to those great personalities of the remote past who seem to us the more transcendent because it was their divinely inspired mission to endow a still-clairvoyant people with those priceless blessings that are evident throughout all cultural activity in which we now play our part. Such noble spirits in human form as Zarathustra and Hermes at once claim and rivet our attention. They appear to us so exalted and so glorious because it was THEY who, in the dim dawn of human life, gave to humankind those first most potent and uplifting impulses. The old Egyptian sage had this sublime concept in mind when he spoke to Solon concerning "doctrines gray with age."

✳ ✳ ✳

ADDENDUM

This lecture was delivered in Berlin on February 16, 1911. Since then, external science has probed further into the secrets of that highly advanced primal civilized life in the valley of the Euphrates to which reference has been made on page 65. The following brief outline will indicate some of the results of archaeological research carried out in Mesopotamia at the site of the ancient city known as Ur of the Chaldees. Important discoveries have been made at this place in connection with ancient Euphratean civilization, as the outcome of a joint expedition arranged by the British Museum and the Museum of the University of Pennsylvania in 1922 under the direction of C. Leonard Woolley. In a lecture given before the Royal Society of Arts on November 8, 1933 and that appeared in their journal, Dr. Woolley said: "Certainly the discoveries that we made at Ur in the last ten years have tended to set scientists by the ears rather than satisfying them with the new information obtained. . . . Few surprises in recent years have been so great as that occasioned by the excavation of the great cemetery lying beneath the ruins of Ur."

In the vaulted chambers of rubble masonry in the tombs of kings, dating as far back as 3500 B.C.E., were found treasures of gold, silver, mosaic, and others, made by the Sumerian workers and of a degree of technical excellence unsurpassed by the craftsmen of today. In one case, when referring to an especially fine specimen of polychrome art that is now known as the *Ram Caught in a Thicket*, Dr. Woolley drew attention to the fact that this particular sculpture, while characteristic of the work of the ancients in 3400 B.C.E. in the Near East. was actually suggestive of that of some rather late Italian Renaissance artist. As the investigations proceeded, it became abundantly clear that the ancient people who had so skill-fully fashioned the strange and wonderful treasures brought to light "were not tyros [novices]; they must have had behind them long traditions, long apprenticeship."

With the view of obtaining insight into the history of this bygone and highly developed civilization, excavations were commenced at a point that was actually the ground level of 3200 B.C.E.; there, through a depth of over sixty feet, relics of the dim past were unearthed in clearly marked strata. Traces of eight superimposed cities were revealed, and deep down beneath the remains of an ancient pottery factory—so Dr. Woolley tells us— the excavators "suddenly came upon a mass, eleven feet thick, of water-laid sand and clay, perfectly uniform and clean, which was undoubtedly the silt thrown up by" the Flood. "We can," said Dr. Woolley, "actually connect it with the flood which we call Noah's Flood." The verge of this deluge was found to be up "against the flank of the mound on which stood the earliest and most primitive city of Ur." Below this deposit were "the remains of antediluvian houses . . . the lowest human buildings rested upon black organic soil . . . and that in turn went down below sea-level."

The excavations proved that the ancient Sumerian architects were familiar with concrete at the beginning of the fourth millennium B.C.E. and possibly earlier. They were acquainted with every basic form of modern architecture, and Dr. Woolley further states that there is no doubt that "the arch, the vault, the apse, and the dome, used in Europe for the first time in the Roman period"—specimens of which were found among the ruins—"are a direct inheritance from the Sumerian peoples of the fourth millennium B.C.E. *at least, and they may well go back to a date still more remote*" [italics added]. Further, it has been shown that continuity in Sumerian civilization undoubtedly extended from the fifth millennium B.C.E. up to the sixth century B.C.E. This fact has come to light as a result of discoveries made by digging beneath the foundations of the massive staged tower known as the Ziggurat of Ur, the main religious building of the city, and by tracing the dates and character of cylinder seals of different periods, carried by these bygone peoples for the purpose of signing written documents.

Toward the close of his most interesting lecture, Dr. Woolley stated that imports into Egypt before the First Dynasty seemed to indicate that the Sumerians imparted to the then-barbarous people of that country an impulse that enabled them to develop their remarkable civilization. He further said: "Civilized as the Babylonians were, they made no new discoveries at all; they hardly advanced beyond what their predecessors had known, and they preserved civilization rather than invented it. We know, too, that the Sumerians sent out the ancestors of the Hebrews with all the traditions of law, civilization, religion and art, which they had themselves enjoyed in their home country and which the Hebrews never entirely forgot, but by which they were profoundly influenced."

Thus has this joint archaeological expedition, under the able leadership of Dr. Woolley, thrown the light of modern external science upon one of those glorious spiritual civilizations of the dim gray past, so often referred to by Rudolf Steiner, which endured just so long as its people opened their hearts to the guidance of the spirit but fell away and perished when they left the true path and gave themselves up to material things. [Ed.]

3. BUDDHA

IN THESE DAYS there is much discussion concerning the Buddha and the Buddhist creed; this fact is the more interesting to all who follow the course of human evolution because a knowledge of the true character of the Buddhist religion, or perhaps more correctly the longing felt by many for its comprehension, has only recently entered into the spiritual life of the Western nations. Let us consider for a moment that most prominent personality Johann Wolfgang von Goethe, who exerted such a powerful influence on Western culture at the turn of the eighteenth and nineteenth centuries, which influence continued so potently right on into our own period. When we examine his life, his works, and his intellectuality, we find no trace of the Buddhist doctrine. A little later, however, we note in the concepts of that genius Arthur Schopenhauer (who was in a certain sense a disciple of Goethe) a clear and definite touch of Buddhistic thought, and since that period in which Schopenhauer lived the interest taken in Eastern spiritual conceptions has steadily increased. Hence it is that there is now a widespread and inherent desire to analyze and discuss all those matters connected with the name of the Great Buddha that have found their way into the course of human evolution.

It is a remarkable fact that most people still persist in associating Buddhism primarily with the idea of recurrent earth lives, to which concept we have often referred in these lectures. Such an assumption is, however, found to be unwarranted when we regard the essential character of Buddhist belief. We might say that with the majority of those people who interest themselves in this subject the notion of repeated earth lives or, as we term it, reincarnation forms a well-established and essential part of their preconceived ideas regarding Buddhism. But on the other hand it must be said, even though it sounds grotesque, that to those who probe more deeply into these matters the association of Buddhism with the idea of reincarnation appears almost equivalent to saying that the most complete knowledge of ancient works of art is to be sought among those peoples who have destroyed them at the commencement of universal development and progress in the Middle Ages. This certainly sounds grotesque, but it is nevertheless true, as we at once realize when we consider that the aim of Buddhism is directed toward the disparagement of our apparently inevitably recurring earth lives and the reduction of their number as far as may be within our power. So we must regard as the essential moving principle underlying the whole trend of Buddhist spiritual thought that principle which operates in the direction of freedom, that is, redemption from repeated rebirth or liberation from reincarnation, which it accepts as an established and unquestionable fact; in this concept is expressed the true and vital essence of Buddhism.

Even from a superficial glance at the history of Western spiritual life we learn that the idea of repeated earthly existence is quite independent of an understanding of Buddhism and vice versa, for during the course of our Western spiritual development we find ourselves confronted with a conception of reincarnation, presented in a manner both lofty and sublime by a personality who most certainly remained untouched by Buddhist views and trend of thought. This personality was Gotthold Lessing, who in his treatise *The Education of Humankind*, which is regarded as the most mature and mellow of his works, closes with the confession that he himself was a believer in the doctrine of reincarnation. With regard to this belief, he gives expression to those deeply significant words "Is not all eternity mine?" Lessing was of the opinion that the repetition of our earthly lives was proof that benefit would accrue from mundane endeavor and that existence in this world is not in vain. For while we toil, we look forward to ever-widening and fuller recurring corporal states in which we may bring to maturity the fruits of our bygone earthly lives. The conception that Lessing really formed was of the prospect and anticipation of a rich and bountiful harvest to be garnered in the fullness of time coupled with the knowledge that throughout human existence there is ever an inner voice that in actual expectation of recurrent earth lives calls to us, saying, "Thou shalt persist in thy labours." From what has been said, it is now apparent that it is in the very essence of Buddhism that human beings must strive to obtain such knowledge and wisdom as may serve to free them from those future reincarnations, the prevision of which lies in the spirit. Only when, during one of our earth lives, we have at last freed ourselves from the need of experiencing those that would otherwise follow can we enter peacefully upon that condition which we may term Eternity.

I have persistently endeavored to make it clear that the idea of reincarnation, both with regard to spiritual science and

Theosophy, was not derived from any one of the ancient traditions, not even from Buddhism; it has in fact thrust itself upon us during our time as a result of independent observation and reflection concerning life in connection with spiritual investigation. To associate Buddhism so directly with the idea of reincarnation indicates a superficial attitude. If we would indeed look into the true character and nature of Buddhism, then we must turn our spiritual eyes in quite another direction.

I must now once again draw your attention to that law in human evolution which we met with when we were considering the personality of the great Zarathustra. In accordance with this law, as was then stated, during the gradual passing of time the whole condition and character of the human soul changed, while it went through varying transitional states. Those events regarding which we obtain information from external historical documents represent, as far as the human being is concerned, only a comparatively late phase in the evolution of humanity. If, however, we look back with the aid of spiritual science to prehistoric times, we gain much more knowledge; we then find that a certain condition of soul was common to the primitive human being, whereby the normal state of human consciousness was quite other than that of our day.

The preeminently intellectual order of consciousness that leads to the manner in which, during the course of our normal human life, we now regard all things around us—combining them by means of our mental powers acting through the brain, so that they shall be connected with and become a part of our wisdom and our science—was first developed from another form of conscious state. I have emphasized this point before, but I must lay particular stress upon it once again. We have in the chaotic disorder of our dream life a last remnant—a species of atavistic heritage—of an old clairvoyance, which was at one time and to a certain extent an ordinary condition of the human soul and in which humankind assumed a state between that of sleeping and that of being awake; humans could then look upon those things hidden behind the perceptual world.

In these days in which our consciousness mainly alternates between the sleeping and the waking conditions, it is only in the latter that we seek to apprehend a state of intellectuality in the soul. In olden times, however, clairvoyant visions were not so meaningless as are the dream forms of our period, for they could be quite definitely ascribed to specific superperceptual creations and events. Humankind had in connection with these ancient fluctuating visions a species of conscious state out of which our present intellectuality gradually evolved. Thus, we look back to a certain form of primeval clairvoyance that was followed by the long-drawn-out evolution of our consciousness as recognized today. Because of this bygone dreamlike clairvoyance, prehistoric human beings could gaze far into the superperceptual worlds and through this connection with the supersensible they gained not knowledge alone but also a feeling of profound inner satisfaction and bliss from the full realization of the soul's union with the spirit world.

Just as present-day human beings are now convinced through sense perceptions and intellectuality that the blood is composed of substances that exist outside in the physical universe, so were prehistoric human beings confident that their soul and spiritual nature emanated from that same hidden spirit world which they could discern by virtue of clairvoyant consciousness.

It has already been pointed out that there are phenomena connected with the history of humankind, and which are also
apparent in certain external facts and happenings, that can be
fully understood only when we presuppose some such primordial condition of human earthly existence. It has further been
stated that modern science is coming more and more to the
conclusion that it is erroneous to assume, as has been done by
the materialistic anthropology of the nineteenth century, that
in primeval times the prevailing state common to human
beings was similar to that found among the most primitive
peoples of today. It is, in fact, becoming more and more clear
that the prehistoric races had extremely exalted theoretical conceptions regarding the spirit world and that these concepts
were given to them in the form of visions. All those curious
ideas that come to us through myths and legends can be rightly
understood only when they are first connected with and
referred back to the ancient wisdom that came to humankind
in a way wholly different from that by which our present intellectual science has been attained.

In these modern times there is not much sympathy expressed
with the view that the position in which we find the primitive
peoples of our day is not typical of the universal primordial
condition of humankind but is in reality an example of decadence from a primarily highly clairvoyant spiritual state common to all peoples. But facts will yet force a general acceptance
of some such hypothesis as that put forward by spiritual science as a result of its investigations. Here, as in many other
cases, it can be shown that fundamentally there is complete
accord between spiritual and external science. Further, a time
will come when the conclusions that spiritual science has
formed regarding the probable future of human evolution,

viewed from the scientific standpoint, will be entirely confirmed. We must look back not merely to a form of primeval
wisdom but indeed to a specific order of primordial feeling
and apprehension, which we characterize as a clairvoyant bond
once existing between human beings and the divine regions of
spirit.

We can easily understand that during the transition from the
old or clairvoyant state of the human soul to our modern
direct, unprejudiced, and intellectual method of regarding the
external perceptual world, there should arise two different currents of thought. As time went on, the first of these currents
manifested more especially among those peoples who had
clung to memories of the past and to their fading psychic
power, in such manner that they would say, "In bygone days
humankind was truly in contact with the spirit realms through
the clairvoyant faculty, but since then human beings have
descended into the material world of sense perception." This
feeling spread throughout the whole soul's outlook, until those
ancient peoples would cry out, "We are indeed now come into
a world of manifestations where all is illusion, all is maya."
Only at such time as human beings might commune with the
spirit spheres could they truly comprehend and be united with
their very being. Thus it was that there came to those nations
that still preserved a dim remembrance of the ancient primal
clairvoyant state a certain feeling of sadness at the thought of
what they had lost and an indifference to all material things
that human beings might apprehend and understand through
the medium of the intellect and with which they are ever in
direct and conscious contact.

On the other hand, the second of the two thought currents to
which I have referred may be expressed in the following manner:

"We will observe and be active in this new world that has been given to us." Thought of this nature is especially noticeable throughout the Zarathustran doctrine. Those who experienced this call to action did not look back with sorrow and longing to the loss of the old clairvoyant power but felt more and more that they must keep in close and constant touch with those forces by the aid of which they might penetrate into the secrets and nature of all material things, knowing full well that knowledge and guidance, born of the spirit, would flow in upon them if they would but give themselves up to earnest and profound meditation and piety. Such people felt impelled to link themselves closely with the world—there was no dreaming of the past but instead an urge to gaze resolutely into the future and to battle with what might come. They expressed themselves after this fashion: "Interwoven throughout this world, which is now our portion, is the same divine essence that was spread about us and permeated our very beings in bygone ages; this spiritual component we must now seek amid our material surroundings. It is our task to unite ourselves with all that is good and of the spirit and, by so doing, to further the progress and evolution of creation." These words indicate the essential nature of the current of thought that was occupied with external physical perception and went forth from those Asiatic countries where the Zarathustran doctrine prevailed, which lay northward of the region where humankind looked back in meditation, pondering over that great spiritual gift that had passed away and was indeed lost.

Thus it came about that upon the soil of India there arose a spiritual life that is entirely comprehensible when we regard it in the light of all this retrospection concerning a former union with the spirit world. If we consider the results in India of the teachings of the Sankhya and Yoga philosophies and the Yoga training, we find that these may be embodied in the following statement: "Indians have ever striven to reestablish their connection with those spirit worlds from whence they came, and it has been their constant endeavor to eliminate from their earthly life all that was spread around them in external creation and by thus freeing themselves from material things to regain their union with that spiritual region from whence humanity has emanated. The principle underlying Yoga philosophy is reunion with the divine realms and abstraction from all that appertains to the perceptual world."

Only when we assume this fundamental mood of Indian spiritual life can we realize the significance of that mighty impulse brought about by the advent of the Buddha, which blazed up before our spiritual sight as an afterglow across the evening sky of Indian soul life just a few centuries before the Christ impulse began to dominate Western thought. It is only in the light of the Buddha mood, when regarded as character-ized here, that the outstanding figure of the Buddha can be truly comprehended. In view of that basic assumption to which we have referred, we can readily conceive that in India there could exist an order of thought and conviction such as caused humankind to regard the world as having fallen from a spiritual state into one of sense illusion, or the "Great Decep-tion" that is indeed maya. It is also understandable that Indi-ans, because of their observations concerning this external world with which humanity is so closely connected, pictured to themselves that this decline came about suddenly and unexpectedly from time to time during the passing of the ages. So that Indian philosophy does not regard the fall of humanity as uniform and continuous but rather as having taken place periodically from epoch to epoch. From this point of view we can now understand those contemplative moods underlying a form of culture that we must regard as being in the departing radiance of its existence; for so must we characterize the Buddhist conception if we would consider it as having a place in a philosophy such as we have outlined.

Indian thought ever harked back to that dim past when humans were truly united with the spirit world. For there came a time when Indians fell away from their exalted spiritual standard; this decline persisted until a certain level was reached, when they rose again only to sink once more. They continued to alternate in this fashion throughout the ages, every descent taking them still further along the downward path while each upward step was, as it were, a mitigation granted by some higher power, in order that humans might not be compelled to work and live all too suddenly in the condition that they had already entered upon during their fall. According to ancient Indian philosophy, as each period of decline ended there arose a certain outstanding figure whose personality was known as a "Buddha"; the last was incarnated as the son of King Suddhodana, and called Gautama Buddha.

Since those olden times, when humanity was still directly united with the spirit world, there have arisen a number of such Buddhas, five having appeared subsequent to the last fall. The advent of the Buddhas was a sign that humankind will not sink into illusion—into maya—but that again and again there will come into human beings' lives something of the ancient primal wisdom to succor and aid humanity. Because of human beings' constant downward trend, however, their primordial knowledge fades from time to time. In order that it shall be renewed, there arises periodically a new Buddha; the last was Gautama Buddha.

Before such great teachers could advance through repeated earth lives to the dignity of Buddhahood, if we may so express it, they must have already been exalted and attained the lofty standing of a Bodhisattva.[5] According to the Indian philosophical outlook, up to his twenty-ninth year Gautama Buddha was not regarded as a Buddha but as a Bodhisattva. It was therefore as a Bodhisattva that he was born into the royal house of Suddhodana. Because his life was ever devoted to toil and to striving, he was at last blessed with that inner illumination symbolically portrayed in the words "sitting under the Bodhi tree," and the glorious enlightenment that flowed in upon him found expression in the Sermon at Benares.

Thus did Gautama Buddha rise to the full dignity of Buddhahood in his twenty-ninth year. From that time on he was empowered to revive once again a last remnant of bygone primeval wisdom, which in the light of Indian conceptions would be destined to fall into decadence during the centuries to come. But according to these same concepts, when human beings have sunk so low that the wisdom and the knowledge which this last Buddha brought shall have waned, then will yet another Bodhisattva rise to Buddhahood, the Buddha of the Future—the Maitreya Buddha whose coming the Indians surely await, for it is foretold in their philosophy.

Let us now consider what took place at that time when the last Bodhisattva rose to Buddhahood, when, as we might say, his soul became filled with primordial wisdom. In this way we can best realize and understand the true significance of that great change, wrought by struggle and toil through repeated

---

5. Bodhisattva (Sanskrit). A Bodisat, one whose essence is enlightenment, that is, one destined to become a Buddha. A Buddha Elect.

Buddha's Life

earth lives. There is a legend that tells us that until his twenty-ninth year he had seen nothing of the world outside the royal palace of Suddhodana and that he was protected from the misery and suffering that are factors of existence ever antagonistic to human prosperity in life's progress. It was under these conditions that the Bodhisattva grew up. At the same time, however, he was possessed of the Bodhisattva consciousness, a consciousness imbued with inner wisdom garnered from previous incarnations. Hence, as he developed during his life's unfolding, he looked only upon those things that would bring forth true and goodly fruits. Since this legend is so well known, it is necessary to refer only to the main points. It states that when the Buddha at length went outside the royal palace, he had an experience such as could not have occurred before—namely, he beheld a corpse—and he realized on seeing this body that life is dissolved by death and that the death element breaks in upon life's procreative and fruitful progress. He next came upon an ailing and feeble man and knew that disease enters upon life. Again, he saw an aged person, tottering and weary, and he understood that old age creeps in upon the freshness of youth.

Let us now place ourselves in the position of those who look upon experiences of this nature solely from the Buddhistic point of view, for instance, in the position of this Bodhisattva Gautama. Gautama was possessed of a higher wisdom that lived within him but was as yet not fully developed. He had, up to this period, seen only the fortunate and wealthy side of life; now, for the first time, he beheld the elements of decay and dissolution. If we consider the way in which he must have regarded these happenings, as viewed from the standpoint of assumptions forced upon him by his inner being, we can readily understand how it was that this great spiritual Buddha came to express himself in words somewhat as follows: "When we attain to knowledge and to wisdom, it comes about that by virtue of such wisdom we are led onward toward development and progress. And because of this enlightenment, there enters into the soul the thought of an ever-continuous and beneficial growth and advancement. When we look upon the world about us, however, we see there the elements of destruction as expressed in sickness, old age, and death. Truly it cannot be wisdom that would thus mingle these destructive factors with life but something quite apart and distinctive in character."

At first the great Gautama did not fully grasp all that his Bodhisattva consciousness implied, and we can well understand how it was that he became imbued with those thoughts that caused him to exclaim, "Humans may indeed be possessed of much wisdom, and through their knowledge there may come to them the idea of plenteous benefits. In life, however, we behold around us not alone the factors of sickness and death but indeed many other baneful elements that bring corruption and decay into our very existence." From the persepective of Buddhism, Indian philosophy presupposes that he who was a Bodhisattva and is exalted to Buddhahood regards all such life experiences with the Bodhisattva consciousness. This supposition must be clearly understood. Gautama realized that in the great wisdom underlying development in all being, there is an element destructive to existence. The legend states that when this truth first dawned upon him, his great soul was so affected that he cried out: "Life is full of misery."

The Bodhisattva thus saw around him a condition he could not as yet fully comprehend. He had passed through life after life, always applying the experiences gained through his previous incarnations to his soul's benefit. In the course of these repeated lives his wisdom became greater and greater, till at last he could look down upon all earthly existence from a more exalted vantage point. But when he came forth from the king's palace and saw before him for the first time the realities of life, its true nature and significance did not at once penetrate his understanding. The knowledge that we gain from the repeated experiences of our earth lives and which we store within us as wisdom can never solve the ultimate secrets of our being, for the true origin of these mysteries must lie without—remote from the life that is ours as we pass from reincarnation to reincarnation.

Such thoughts matured in the great soul of Gautama and led him directly to that sublime enlightenment known as "the illumination under the Bodhi tree.[6]" There, while seated beneath this tree, it became clear to the Buddha that this world in which we have our being is maya, or illusion; that here life follows upon life; and that we have come upon this earth from a spiritual realm. While we are here, we may indeed be exalted and even rise to noble heights in the divine sense, and we may pass through many reincarnations, becoming ever more and more possessed of wisdom. Because of that which is material and comes to us through contact with this earthly life, however, we can never solve the great ever-present mystery of existence that finds expression in old age, disease, and death. It was at this time of enlightenment that the thought came to Gautama that the teachings born of suffering held for him a greater significance than all the wisdom of a Bodhisattva.

---

6. Bodhi tree, Fig tree (*Ficus religiosa*); known also as the Bo tree.

The Buddha expressed the fundamental concept underlying his great illumination as follows: "That which spreads itself abroad throughout this world of maya is not wisdom; indeed, so little of this quality is manifested in life that we can never hope to gain from external experiences a true understanding of affliction or acquire the knowledge that will show us the way by which we may be freed from suffering. For interwoven throughout all outer existence is a factor of quite another character, which differs from all wisdom and all knowledge." It is therefore obvious that what the Buddha sought was an element through the agency of which the destructive forces of old age, sickness, and death become commingled with earthly life and in which wisdom has no part. He held that freedom from these baneful factors can never come through mundane knowledge and learning, for the path leading to deliverance does not lie in that direction and can be found only when the human being withdraws entirely from the external world, where life follows upon life and reincarnation upon reincarnation.

Thus it was the Buddha realized from the moment of his illumination that in the teachings and experience born of affliction lay that basic element necessary to humanity for its future progress. He conceived a factor (wherein was no wisdom) that he termed "the thirst for existence" to be the true source of all the misery and sorrow that so trouble the world. Upon the one side there is wisdom and upon the other a thirst for existence, where wisdom has no part. It was this thought that caused Gautama to exclaim, "Only liberation from recurrent earth life can lead humanity to the realization of perfect freedom, for earthly wisdom—even that of the highest learning—cannot save us from grief and anguish." He therefore gave himself up to meditation and sought some means whereby humankind might be led away from all this restlessness in the world of reincarnations and guided into the transcendent state that Gautama Buddha designated Nirvana.

Nirvana

What, then, is the nature of this state—this world of Nirvana—that human beings will enter when they have so advanced in earthly life that the thirst for existence has passed and they no more desire to be reborn? We must understand this concept rightly, for then shall we avoid those grotesque and fantastic ideas so frequently spread abroad. Nirvana is a condition that can be characterized only in the Buddhist sense. According to this conception, it is a world of redemption and bliss that can never be expressed in terms of things that may be apprehended in the material state in which we have our being. There is nothing in this physical world or in the wide expanse of the cosmos that can awaken in humankind a realization of the sublime truth underlying such redemption.

Hence, we should forbear from all pronouncements and assertions regarding that glorious region where humanity must seek salvation. All earth-born predications and profitless statements—such as human beings are ever prone to make—must be stilled, for in them is nothing pertaining to the spheres of eternal bliss. There is, indeed, no possibility of picturing that realm where all may enter who have overcome the need for reincarnation, since it is not of a substance with those things of which we may have awareness in this earthly life. When, therefore, we would speak of this condition, we must use a negative, indefinite term; such a term is Nirvana. Those who have conquered all mundane desires shall yet know the nature and the aspect of that other world which we can but indicate with one vague and neutral word—Nirvana. It is a region that, according to the Buddhist, no language can portray. It is not nihilism; it is indeed so far removed from such a concept that we can find no words wherewith to describe this state of being, so complete, perfect, and all abounding in ecstasy and bliss.

We are now in a position to grasp and apprehend the very essence of Buddhism, its sentiments, and its convictions. From the time of the Sermon at Benares, when the Buddha first gave expression to the doctrine of suffering, Buddhism became permeated with thought and understanding concerning the inner nature of life's misery and distress and of that yearning, that thirst for existence that leads only to sorrow and affliction. There is, according to this doctrine, only one way in which humanity may truly progress, and that is through gaining freedom and redemption from further reincarnations. Humankind must find the path of knowledge that extends outward and beyond all earthly wisdom—the path that is the way and the means whereby slowly and step by step human beings may become so fitted and conditioned that they can at last enter upon the ideal state of Nirvana. In other words, they must learn to utilize the experiences of their rebirths in such way that, finally, recurrent earth life is no longer essential to development and they are freed from it forever.

If we now turn from this brief summary of the conceptions that underlie Buddhism to the root and essence of this religion, it at once strikes us as peculiar when viewed in the light of our ideas concerning humanity regarded as a whole. For Buddhism in point of fact isolates the individual. Questions are raised relative to human destiny, the purport and aim of existence, the place and relation of human beings to the world—all from the standpoint of detached and separate personality. How, indeed, could any other trend of thought underlie a philosophy built upon a fundamental disposition of mind such as we have out-lined? A philosophy evolved from a basic mood that conceives human beings as being descended from spiritual heights and now finding themselves in a world of illusion, from which material existence the wisdom of a Buddha may, from time to time, free him. But this very wisdom (as was seen in the case of the last Buddha) causes him to seek redemption from his earthly life. How could the goal of human existence, born as it was of convictions such as these, be characterized other than by representing humans as isolated in relation to the whole of their environment? According to this philosophy, the funda-mental aspect of being is such as to represent decline, while development and evolution in earthly life implies degeneration.

The manner in which the Buddha sought enlightenment is both remarkable and significant, but unless we consider also the peculiar characteristics and circumstances connected with the "illumination," neither the Buddha himself nor Buddhism can be properly understood. When Gautama craved enlighten-ment, he went forth into solitude to a place where he could find entire and absolute isolation. All that he had acquired from life to life had to be overcome in the utter detachment of his being, so that there could break in upon his soul that clear light whereby he might comprehend and solve the mystery of the world's wretchedness. There, in that place, as one in com-plete aloofness and dependent upon himself alone, the Buddha awaited the moment of illumination—that moment when there should come to him an understanding which would enable him to realize that the true cause of all human suffering lay in the intense longing manifested by individuals to be born again into this material world. Moreover, he understood that this yearning for reincarnation, this thirst for existence, is the fundamental source of all the misery and distress everywhere around us and of those pernicious factors that bring ruin and destruction into our very being.

We cannot rightly comprehend the unusual and singular nature of the Buddha illumination and of the Buddhistic doctrine unless we compare them with the knowledge and experience we have gained through Christianity. Six hundred years after the advent of the Great Buddha, there arose in Christendom a wholly different conception, in which we also find human beings' position relative to the world and all that is around them expressed in definite terms.

Regarding Buddhism and speaking in an abstract and general manner, we can say: "The philosophic outlook concerning the cosmos as set forth in Buddhistic teachings is not treated historically, and this unhistoric method is thoroughly typical of all Eastern countries. These countries have seen one Buddha epoch follow upon another, only to gradually die out and eventually come to an end. Such descriptions as are concerned merely with the human being's descent from higher to lower states do not of themselves constitute what we term history, for the factors of true history would include the upward endeavor of humanity to reach some appointed goal and the nature and possibilities of the human being's association and union with the world as a whole, both in the past and in the future. We would then have veritable history. But Buddhists stand isolated and alone, concerned only with the basic principles of their individual being and always seeking to gain through the conduct of their personal life those powers that may lead to freedom from the thirst for existence, so that having attained to this freedom they may at last win redemption from rebirth.

In Christendom, six hundred years after the Buddha period, the attitude of the individual human being toward the evolution of humanity in general was of quite another kind. Putting aside all prejudice, which is so common a failing throughout the world, we can characterize one particular Christian trend of thought as follows: From the part of the Christian concept founded upon the stories in the Old Testament, it is realized that the ancients were related to the spiritual realms in a manner wholly different from that which was subsequently the case, as is seen in the grand and lofty imagery depicted in Genesis. A curious fact comes to light, namely that in Christendom we find the human being's relation to the world to be of a character entirely unlike that which one obtains in Buddhism. The following may be considered as the Christian's point of view: "Within my being is understanding begotten of the condition of soul that is now mine. Because of the manner in which I observe and comprehend this outer perceptual world, there is born in me wisdom, intelligence, and an aptitude for the practical conduct of life. But I can look back into the distant past, when the human soul was differently conditioned. At that time there came about a circumstance—the fall of the human being—that cannot be regarded simply from the Buddhistic standpoint." This event, which we so often find portrayed in figurative form based upon misconception, the Buddhist believes to be a [natural result of the human being's] descent from divine spiritual heights into a world of maya. This great fall must, however, be looked upon quite differently, for truly characterized it is the fall of human beings [as caused wholly through their own transgression and not due, as the Buddhist thinks, merely to their coming down from a higher spiritual state and entering a world of deception].

Although human beings may have their own opinion concerning this matter, there is one thing we must admit, and that will suffice for the present. In connection with the thought of the fall there is an inner sentiment that causes the human being to exclaim, "As I am now, there work within me certain impulses and forces that have surely not developed in my being alone, for similar factors were active in a not so very distant past, when they played a part in happenings of such a nature that the human race, to which I belong, not only lapsed from its former higher spiritual standard but indeed fell so far that humankind has come into a different relation with the world than the one that would have been if the original conditions had but endured."

When human beings fell away from their previous high spiritual state, they sank to a definitely lower level, and this change was brought about by what may be termed their own conscious sin. We are therefore not concerned merely with the fact of descent, as is the case when the fall is viewed from the Buddhist perspective, for we must take into consideration varying moods during this period of decadence. If human beings' first nature had continued unchanged, this decline would not have the character it has now assumed, where the soul state is such that they are always prone to fall into temptation.

Those who penetrate beneath the surface of Christianity and study deeply learn that while history ran its course, human soul quality altered. In other words, because of certain events that happened in ancient times, the human soul (the working of which may be likened to a subconscious mind within one's being) took to itself a quality quite unlike that which was originally intended. Buddhists' position relative to the material world may be expressed differently. A Buddhist would say, "I have been taken out of a divine spiritual realm and placed upon this earth; when I look around me I find nothing but illusion—all is maya." The Christian, on the other hand, would say, "When I came down into this material life, had I but conformed to the order and intent of that divine plan in which I had my part, I could even now look beyond this perceptual pretence, behind all this deception, this maya, and I would at all times have the power to realize and discern that which is genuine and true. Because my deeds were not in harmony with those things that had been ordained when I descended upon this earth, I have, through my own act, caused this world to become an illusion."

To the question "Why is this world one of maya? the Buddhist answers thus: "It is the world itself that is maya." But the Christian says: 'It is I who am at fault, I alone; my limited capacity for discernment and my whole soul state have placed me in such a position that I can no more apprehend that which was in the beginning. And my actions and conduct have ceased to be of such a nature that results follow smoothly, ever attended with beneficial and fruitful progress. I myself have enwrapped this material life in a veil of maya." The Buddhist's standpoint is that the world is a great illusion and must be overcome. The Christian says, "I have been placed upon this earth and must here find the purpose and object of my being." When Christians once understand that through spiritual science knowledge may be acquired concerning recurrent earth lives, they then realize that they may use this wisdom for the achievement of the true aim of existence. They become convinced that the reason why we now look upon a world of sorrow and deception is that we have wandered from our allotted path. They consider that this change to maya is the direct result of human deeds and the manner in which they regard the world. Christians, therefore, are of the opinion that in order to attain eternal bliss, we must not seek to withdraw ourselves from this earthly state but instead master the condition that we alone have brought about and through which the aspect of all material things has been transformed into one of illusion, such that we no longer apprehend them in their truth and reality. We must overcome this deception; then may we follow the course of our first duly appointed destiny—for latent within each one of us abides a higher personality. If this more noble hidden self were not hindered and could but look around upon the world, it would apprehend it in truth; human beings would then no longer continue an existence hampered by sickness and death but lead an everlasting life in all the freshness of youth.

Such, then, is the true inner self that we have veiled—veiled, because in the past we have been associated with a certain event in the world's development the effects of which have continued while the primary impulses still work within us, thus proving that we do not exist isolated and alone. We must not believe that we have been led to our present condition through a thirst for existence common to the individual human; rather must we realize that each one of us is a definite unit in the sum total of humanity and as such must take a share and suffer from the results of any original transgression committed by humankind.

In this way Christians feel they are historically united with the whole human race. While they look into the future, they say, "Through travail and toil I must regain touch with the greater self that because of human beings' fall now lies enshrouded within my being. It is not Nirvana that I must seek, but my more noble Ego. Alone must I find the way back to my true nature, and then will the outer world no longer be an illusion, a vision of unreality, but a world wherein I shall overcome of my own power and effort all sorrow, sickness, and death." While Buddhists would seek freedom from earthly conditions and from rebirth through the struggle with the thirst for existence, Christians seek liberation from their lower personality and look forward to the awakening of a higher self, that more exalted Ego, which they alone have veiled, so that through awakening they may at last apprehend this perceptual world in the light of divine truth.

When we compare those significant words of Saint Paul—"Yet not I, but Christ liveth in me" (Galatians 2:20)—with the wisdom revealed by the Buddha, the contrast is as that between light and darkness. In Saint Paul's words we find expressed that positive knowledge, that definite consciousness, which is always active deep within us and by virtue of which we take our place as human personalities in the world. According to Buddhists, humankind has lapsed from spiritual heights because this material world has pressed them down and implanted in them a thirst for existence. This desire they must overcome—they must away! Christians, on the other hand, say, "No! The world is not to blame because of our present state; the fault lies with us alone."

We Christians dwell upon this earth equipped with our accustomed consciousness, but beneath all awareness and understanding there is a something active in each individual personality that in olden times found expression in the form of clairvoyant visioned consciousness, no more extant; even while we possessed this faculty, we transgressed. If we would indeed reach the ultimate goal of our existence, then must we first atone for this human error. No human being who is advanced in years may say, "In my early life I sinned; it is unjust that I should now be called upon to make atonement for youthful faults, committed at a time when I had not yet attained to that fuller knowledge which is now mine." It would be equally wrong to assert that it is unfair to be expected to use our present conscious power to such end that we may compensate for misdeeds enacted while in possession of a different conscious faculty, which faculty no longer exists, for it has been replaced by an intellectual cognition.

The only way in which humans may truly atone, when indeed the will is there, is for them to raise themselves upward from their present conscious state and existing Ego to a higher plane of personality—a more exalted "I." Those words of Saint Paul—"Yet not I, but Christ liveth in me"—could then be characterized as "Yet not I, but a higher consciousness liveth in me." The Christian conception can be expressed in these words: "I have fallen from a higher spiritual state and have entered upon a different condition from that which was previously ordained. But I must rise again, and this I must do not through the quality of Ego that is mine but by virtue of a power that can enter into my very being, uplifting me far above the 'I' that I now possess. Such a change can alone come to pass when the Christ influence is once more active within, leading me onward until the world has lost all power of illusion and I can apprehend it in its true reality. Ever upward must I strive until those baneful forces that have brought sickness and death upon the earth may be vanquished—conquered by the higher spiritual power Christ has brought to life within my being."

The innermost essence of Buddhism is best understood by comparing the Buddhist creed with that of Christianity. We at

once realize why it was that Lessing should have made use of
the phrase "Is not all Eternity mine?" in his book entitled *The
Education of Humankind*. These words imply that if we employ
the experiences gained during our repeated reincarnations in
such a way as to allow the Christ force to abide more and more
within us, we shall at last reach the eternal spheres—which
realms we cannot as yet hope to attain because we have of our
own act enveloped the inner being as with a veil. The idea of
reincarnation will present a wholly different aspect when illumined by the glory of Christianity, but it is not merely the
actual belief in rebirth that matters for the present. For with
the advance of Christian culture, humanity will gradually be
driven to the acceptance of this concept as a truth brought forward by spiritual science.

It is important that we should realize that whereas the deepest sentiments and convictions of the Buddhist faith cause
Buddhists to blame the world for everything that is maya,
Christians, on the other hand, look upon themselves and
humankind in general as responsible for all earthly deception
and illusion. They store within their innermost being those
qualities prerequisite and necessary to rise to the state we term
Redemption. In the Christian sense, however, this does not
imply only deliverance but actual resurrection. For when
human beings have attained to this state, the Ego is raised to
the level of that more exalted "I" from which we have fallen.
When Buddhists look upon the world, they find themselves
concerned with original sin but feel that they have been placed
upon this earth merely for a time; they therefore desire freedom. Christians likewise realize their connection with original
sin but seek amendment and to atone for this first transgression. Such is the historical line of thought, for while Christians

feel that their present existence is associated with an incident that took place in olden times among the ancients, they also connect their lives with an event that will surely come to pass when they are so advanced that their whole being will shine forth, filled with that radiance we designate as the essence of the Christ-being.

Thus it is that during the world's development we find nothing in Christianity corresponding to successive Buddha epochs coming one after another, as one might say unhistorically— each Buddha proclaiming a like doctrine. Christianity brings forward but one single glorious event during the whole of human earthly progress. In the same way as the Buddhist pictures the Buddha seated isolated and alone under the Bodhi tree, at the moment when he was exalted and the great illumination came to him, so does the Christian visualize Jesus of Nazareth at that time when there descended upon him the all-inspiring spirit of the cosmos. The baptism of Christ by John, as described in the Bible, is as vivid and clear a picture as the Buddhist's conception of the illumination of the Buddha. Thus we have, in the first case, the Buddha seated under the Bodhi tree and concerned only with his own soul; in the second, we have Jesus of Nazareth standing in the Jordan while there descended upon him that cosmic essence, that spirit symbolically represented as a dove, which entered into his innermost being.

To those who profess Buddhism, there is something about the Buddha and his works that is as a voice saying, "Thou shalt still this thirst for earthly existence, tear it out by the roots, and follow the Buddha on to those realms that no earthly words can describe." Christians have a similar feeling with regard to the life and example of Christ, for there seems to come forth an influence that makes it possible for them to atone for that primeval deed committed by ancient humanity. They know that when, in their souls, the divine cosmic influence (born of the great spiritual world that lies behind this perceptual earth) becomes as great a living force as in the Christ himself, then will they carry into future reincarnations the increasing realization of the truth of Saint Paul's words "Yet not I, but Christ liveth in me." They will then be raised more and more ever upward to that divine state from which they have fallen. When such a faith is ours, we cannot help but be deeply moved when we hear the story of how the Buddha, as he addressed his intimate disciples, spoke to them as follows: "When I look back upon my former lives as I might look into an open book, where I can read page after page and review each life in turn that is passed, I find in every one of these earthly existences that I have built for myself a material body in which my spirit has dwelt as in a temple. But I now know that this same body in which I have become Buddha will in truth be the last." Speaking of that Nirvana into which he would so soon enter, the Buddha said, "I already feel that the beams are cracking and the supports giving way, that this physical body that has been raised up for the last time will soon be wholly and finally destroyed."

Let us compare these words with the words of Christ as recorded in the Gospel of John (2:19), when Jesus, intimating that he lived in a body that was external and apart, said: "Destroy this temple, and in three days I will raise it up." Here we have an exactly opposite point of view, which might be interpreted thus: "I will perform a deed that will enliven and make fruitful all that in this world is of God and has come down to human beings from primeval times and entered into their being." These words imply that Christians, during recurrent earth lives, must exercise every faculty in order to give truth to the affirmation "Yet not I, but Christ liveth in me." We must, however, clearly understand that Christ's reference to the rebuilding of the temple has an eternal significance and means that the Christ power enters into and is absorbed by all who truly realize that they themselves must play a constructive part in the collective evolution of humanity. It is entirely wrong to speak of the event that gave rise to what we term the Christ impulse as though we anticipated its recurrence in some form during the further development of humankind.

When Buddhists ponder in accordance with the true concepts of their creed, they picture the advent of several Buddhas, appearing one after another throughout recurring Buddha epochs, all of which during the course of their earth lives had a similar character and significance. Christians look back to a single past event described as the fall of human beings through sin, while they point to its converse in the Mystery of Golgotha. They who believe that the Christ event will at some later period be repeated merely show that they have not grasped the true essence of the historical evolution of humankind. History tells us that this idea has been frequently put forward in the past, and it is likely that it will again reappear in the future.

The course of true history must always be dependent upon a single basic event. Just as the arm of a balance must have one point of equilibrium and the beam from which the scales hang have just one point of support, so in the case of a true record of the evolution of humankind there must be a single circumstance to which its historical development (taken either backward or forward) always points. It is as absurd to speak of a repetition of the Christ event as it would be to assert that the beam of a balance could be supported and swing upon two points. That Eastern wisdom should hold to the belief that a number of similar spiritual personalities succeed each other at intervals, as it does in the case of the Buddhas, is characteristic of the difference existing between the Eastern cosmic conception and that which has sprung up among the Western countries as the result of so much painstaking observation and thought concerning the course of evolution. The Western concept first began to take definite form at the time of the manifestation of the Christ impulse, which we must regard as a unique circumstance. If we oppose the oneness and singular character of the Christ event, we argue against the possibility of the true historical evolution of humankind, and to argue against historical evolution betrays a misunderstanding of genuine history.

In its deepest sense, we can term that consciousness possessed by individual human beings of indissoluble association with humanity as a whole as the Christian consciousness. Through it we become aware of a definite purpose underlying the course of all human evolution and realize that here indeed can be no mere repetition. Such consciousness is an attribute of Christianity, from which it cannot be separated. The real progress that humankind has made during its period of development is shown in the advance from the ancient Eastern cosmic conception to the philosophic concept of modern times—from the unhistoric to the historic, from a belief that the wheels of human chance roll on through a succession of similar events to a conviction that underlying the whole of human evolution is a definite purpose, a design of profound significance.

We realize that it is Christianity that first revealed the true meaning of the doctrine of reincarnation. We can now state that the reason why humans must experience recurrent earth lives is so that they may be again and again instilled with the true import of material existence; with this object they are confronted with a different aspect of being during each incarnation. There is throughout humanity an upward tendency that is not confined merely to the isolated individual but extends to the entire human race with which we feel ourselves so intimately connected. The Christ impulse, the center of all, causes us to realize that humans can become conscious of the glory of this divine relationship. Then no more will they acknowledge only the creed of Buddha, who cries out to him, "Free thyself!" They will become aware of their union with the Christ, whose deed has reclaimed them from the consequences of that decadence symbolically represented as the fall of the human being through sin.

We cannot describe Buddhism better than by showing that it is the afterglow of a cosmic conception, the sun of which has nearly set. But with the advent of Gautama it shone forth with one last brilliant, powerful ray. We revere the Buddha nonetheless; we honor him as a Great Spirit—as one whose voice called into the past and brought back into this earthly life once again that mood which brings with it so clear a consciousness of the human connection with ancient primordial wisdom. On the other hand, we know that the Christ impulse points resolutely toward the future, penetrating more and more deeply into the very soul of the human being so that humanity may realize that it is not release and freedom that it should seek but Resurrection—that glorious transfiguration of our earthly being. It is in such a metamorphosis that we find the inner

meaning of our material life. It is futile to search among dog-
mas, concepts, and ideas for the active principle of existence,
for the vital element of life lies in our impulses, emotions, and
feelings; it is through these moods that we may apprehend the
true significance of human evolution and development.

There may be some who feel themselves more drawn toward
Buddhism than toward Christianity, and we must admit that
even in our time there is something about Buddhism that
inspires a certain sympathy in many minds and which is, to a
certain extent, in the nature of a Buddha mood or disposition.
Such a feeling, however, did not exist with Goethe, who sought
to free himself from the pains he endured as a result of the nar-
rowmindedness he found everywhere about him at the time of
his first sojourn in Weimar. His endeavor in this respect was
wholly due to his love of life and his conviction that interwoven throughout all external being is the same spiritual essence
that is the true origin of the divine element in human beings.
Goethe strove to achieve this liberation from distress through
observation of the outer world, going from plant to plant,
from mineral to mineral, and from one work of art to
another—always seeking that underlying spirit from which the
human soul emanates. At the same time, he sought to unify
himself with the divine essence that manifests throughout all
external things.

In conversation with Schopenhauer regarding the influence
of Schopenhauer's thoughts and ideas upon his pupil, Goethe
once said, "When your carefully considered and worthy conceptions come into contact with a wholly different trend of
thought, they will be found at variance with one another."
Schopenhauer had established a maxim expressed in his
often-repeated words as follows: "Life is precarious, and it is

through deep meditation that I seek to alleviate its burdens."
What he really sought was the illumination that would reveal
and make clear the true origin [and intent] of existence. It was
therefore only natural that Buddhist concepts should enter his
mind and mingle with his ideas, causing him to ponder upon
this old creed.

During the progress of the nineteenth century the different
branches of human culture have yielded such great and
far-reaching results that the mind of humans seems incapable
of adjusting in harmony to the flood of new ideas that continually pour in upon it as a consequence of effort expended in
scientific research. The mind feels more and more helpless
before the enormous mass of facts that is the unceasing product of such investigations. We have found this vast world of
accepted truths to be wonderfully in accord with the concepts
of spiritual science, but it is noteworthy that although human
beings' reasoning powers increased greatly during the last century, nevertheless they soon failed to keep pace with the
immense inflow of scientific data. Thus it was that just toward
the close of the nineteenth century and the beginning of the
twentieth century, human beings realized that they could not
hope to understand and master all this new knowledge by
means of the human intellect alone. Everything about us is
connected with and extends into the cosmos and the world of
spirit—and this outer realm is still beyond the limits of human
beings' normal faculties of comprehension. They must therefore seek another way, some as yet untrodden path.

Thus it is that humankind has sought a cosmic philosophy
not wholly at variance with all those facts coming from the
outer world and that make inward appeal to the soul. Spiritual
science is based upon the most profound conceptions and

experiences of divine wisdom and is ever ready to deal with all fresh truths and data brought forward by external science, to assimilate them, and throw new light upon their significance, showing at the same time that in all that exists in external life is embodied the divine essence—the spirit. There are some people, however, who find the concepts of spiritual science inconvenient and unsuitable. They turn away from the world of reality, which demands so much thought and effort for its unfoldment, and, according to their own knowledge and personal ideas, seek a higher plane merely through the development of their individual souls. Thus we have what may be termed an "unconscious Buddhism," which has long existed and has been active in the philosophies of the nineteenth and twentieth centuries. When so-called unconscious Buddhists come into contact with true Buddhism, then, because of indolence and inertia, they feel themselves more at home with this Eastern creed than with European spiritual science, which comes to grips with widespread facts because it knows that throughout the entire range of reality the divine spirit is ever manifest.

There is no doubt that the present sympathy and interest evinced with regard to Buddhism is due in part to feebleness of will and want of faith, born of undeveloped spiritual knowledge. The whole essence of the Christian cosmic conception, which seems to have been in Goethe's mind, demands that human beings shall not give way to their own weak spiritual understanding and talk of the limitations of human knowledge but feel that there is within them something that will carry them above all illusion and bring them to truth and reality, freeing them forever from terrestrial existence. A cosmic conception of this nature may call for much patient resignation, but such is of quite a different order from that which shrinks before the contemplation of the limits of human understanding. Resignation, in the Kantian sense, implies that humankind is altogether incapable of penetrating the deep secrets of the cosmos, and its chief feature lies in the special acknowledgment of the feebleness of human comprehension. That of Goethe is of a different character and is expressed in these words: "You have not yet come so far that you can apprehend the universe in all its glorious reality, but you are capable of developing yourself." Resignation of this kind leads on to that stage of growth and progress when human beings will truly be in a position to call forth the Christ nature from within their being; they yield because they realize that the highest point of their mundane development has not yet been attained. Such an attitude is noble and fully in accord with human understanding. It implies that we pass from life to life with the consciousness of being, looking forward into the future in the knowledge that with regard to recurrent earthly existence all eternity is ours.

Goethe, led on by his truly Christian impulse, regarded the world after the manner of his character Faust. When we cease to look about us in a trivial mood and when we truly realize that all material works must perish and death at last overtake the body, then with Goethe we can say, "If we take heed and ponder our earthly activities, there will come knowledge born of experience, teaching us that while all those things wrought and accomplished in this world must pass away, that which we have built up within ourselves through toil and striving during our contact with the school of earthly life shall not perish, for that is indeed everlasting."

When we consider human evolution, we find ourselves confronted with two modern currents of thought, each leading to a different cosmic conception. One, due to Schopenhauer, pictures the world with all its misery and suffering as of such a nature that we can realize and appreciate the human being's true position only when we gaze upon the works of the great artists. In these masterpieces we often find portrayed the form and figure of a being who, through asceticism, has attained to something approaching liberation from earthly existence and hovers, as it were, above this lower terrestrial life. Fundamentally, Schopenhauer was of the opinion that in the case of a human being thus freed, retrospection concerning material conditions no longer exists and that herein lies the preeminent characteristic of such liberation. Thus, those who have thus won their way to freedom can truly say, "I am still clothed in my bodily garment, but it has now lost all significance; there is nothing left about me that might in time to come recall my earthly life. I strive upward in anticipation of that state with which I shall gain contact when I have at last wholly overcome the world and all that pertains to it." Of such a nature was the sentiment of Schopenhauer after he had become imbued with those ideas and convictions that Buddhist teaching has spread abroad in the world. So with Faust we think not of how our mundane works may endure but look forward to the fruits that they will bring forth in the course of the soul's eternal life; thus are we carried far out and beyond the narrow confines of the Buddhist creed into a world of thought that finds brief expression in those impressive words of Goethe:

"Eons cannot erase
The traces of my days on earth."

4. MOSES

WHEN WE STUDY the great historical individualities of the past, such as those who have already claimed our attention during these lectures, namely, Zarathustra, Hermes, and Buddha, we are brought face to face with incidents and facts of interest to us as human beings, because we feel that our whole soul life plays a part in the collective evolution of humanity. It is only when we look back to those great spiritual characters of bygone times who have helped to bring about the conditions in which we now live that we can truly comprehend our present circumstances. With regard to Moses, whose personality we are about to consider, the matter presents a wholly different aspect; here we have the feeling that there is no limit to that direct influence exerted by all those events connected with his name that yet continue to affect the spiritual content of our souls. We still feel in our very bones, as it were, the workings of those impulses that emanated from this great, outstanding patriarch. It seems to us that Moses is even now a living force in our thoughts and feelings and as if when we analyze our ideas and motives according to his doctrine and sentiments, we are in truth arraigning and searching our very souls. It is for this reason that all the persistent tradition directly associated with Moses seems to us more vivid, more actually present, than that which is connected with those other great personalities to whom I have referred. It is therefore in a certain sense less difficult to deal with this outstanding individuality, for through the Bible we are all familiar with this mighty figure whose influence has endured even to the present time.

Although the conscientious researches conducted by science during the past ten years and more have to a certain extent touched upon the surface and here and there thrown new light upon the history of Moses—insofar as it can be gleaned from the Bible—when we look more deeply into the matter, we must admit that very little indeed has been altered with regard to the general impression we have received from our own personal study of the scriptures. Whenever we refer to any matter connected with Moses or to the great patriarch himself, we speak as if we were mentioning some subject well known throughout the widest circles; this fact somewhat simplifies the contemplation of the historical features. On the other hand, certain difficulties arise because of the manner in which the Bible tradition concerning Moses is expressed. This we at once comprehend when we call to mind the vicissitudes that accompanied the biblical researches of the nineteenth century.

There is scarcely a single branch of human knowledge or sincere scientific endeavor, even when we include the natural sciences, that claims to so high a degree our deep admiration and reverence as do these investigations. I feel that this point should be repeatedly emphasized. The industry, the discrimination, the devoted and unselfish scientific application expended upon separate sections of the Bible in order to educe from their character and style a definite knowledge of their alleged origin are considered by those who have followed these researches closely as a work that has had no parallel during the nineteenth century.

All this investigation of the past hundred years has, however, a tragic side, for the further the researches were carried, the more did they tend to place the Bible beyond the reach of the people. Those who consult the current literature concerning the results of these exhaustive studies can convince themselves of this fact. The difficulty arose because the Bible was dissected and split up, particularly in the case of the Old Testament, in an attempt to show, for instance, that a certain passage occurring in one part of the Bible owed its origin to a different current of tradition from that of a passage in another part. During this period of time the whole subject matter gradually became welded together in a form that made it necessary for it to be first separated out in this scholarly manner so that it might be understood. In a certain sense, then, the outcome of these investigations must be looked upon as tragic, since they were fundamentally wholly negative in character and contributed nothing toward the continuance of that vivifying influence which the Bible is capable of exerting and which has lived in the hearts and souls of humankind for thousands of years.

The movement toward true spiritual development that we have termed spiritual science is chiefly concerned with constructive activities and is not interested in mere criticism, as is so often the case with other sciences. In our time its most important task is to bring about once again an accurate and proper understanding of the Bible. In this regard it puts forward the following question: "Is it not essential that we should first penetrate into the very depths of the import and significance underlying the whole character of the ancient Biblical traditions and then, only after they are fully and clearly under-stood, inquire as to their origin?" Such a procedure is not easy, especially with reference to the Old Testament, and is particu-larly difficult with respect to those sections dealing with the great outstanding figure and personality of Moses.

We would now ask, "What is it that spiritual science has to say regarding the peculiar nature of those ancient biblical descriptions?" It tells us that those external events associated with this or that personality or nation have been chronicled in the order and manner in which they actually occurred, as viewed from the standpoint of external history. Following this method, the personality of Moses is so depicted that his expe-riences in the physical world are represented just as they took place in relation to space and time. It is only when we have made a profound study of the Bible through the medium of spiritual science that we realize that a biblical description con-cerned with external happenings and experiences may become merged in one of quite another nature; it is often with diffi-culty that we can distinguish this change in fundamental char-acter. We are told, for instance, of journeys and otherworldly events that we accept as such; all unnoticed as the account con-tinues, we then find ourselves confronted with a graphic narra-tive of a wholly different order. It seems to us that a certain journey is represented as continuing from one definite place to another and as if we were expected to look upon the account of events depicted in the latter part of the narrative in the same light as the external physical happenings described at the beginning. In reality, however, the latter part of such an account may actually be a figurative portrayal of the soul life of the particular personality to whom the story has reference. It then has no connection whatever with external worldly events but depicts the soul experiences, struggles, and conquests through which this special being is raised to a higher degree of soul development, greater enlightenment, a more advanced stage of activity, or a mission concerned with the world's evolution. In such a case, descriptions of outside events pass over without any noticeable change directly into pictorial representations, which though they remain similar in style and character have absolutely no significance with regard to external physical happenings but refer only to the inner experiences of the soul.

This assertion will always remain a mere assertion to those who are unable to utilize the methods of spiritual science and thus enter gradually and understandingly into the strange and unusual features associated with many of the graphic narratives found in the Bible. More particularly will this be the case with regard to those sections dealing with the patriarch Moses. When, however, we study this strange method of representation deeply, we notice that when at a certain point in a story the description of external physical events changes into one of soul experiences, the whole style and fundamental character of the account alters, while a new element suddenly makes its appearance. If we ask ourselves, "How does it come about that we are able to perceive this change?" we can answer only that we realize it because of a conviction that comes to us from the soul. This curious descriptive method we have just characterized lies at the base of ancient religious historical narratives, more especially when they are concerned with personalities who have reached a high standard of discernment and understanding of the soul's action and inner workings.

The further we advance and the more deeply we become immersed in the study of spiritual science, the greater is our faith in this singular style of representation. But just because of the strangeness of this method, it is in some ways far from easy to gain a clear comprehension of the true meaning of certain passages that occur in the graphic delineation of Moses. On the one hand we have the Bible with its apparently straightforward narrative, but on the other hand there are difficulties owing to the curious way in which the account is presented when the subject matter is of an especially profound character. This fact has resulted in the customary interpretations being much too liberal in many cases.

When, for instance, we consider the conception of ancient Hebrew history as advanced by the philosopher Philo, who lived at the time of the founding of Christianity, we realize at once that he endeavored to portray the whole record of the old Hebrew nation as if it were an allegory. Philo aimed at a figurative representation in which the entire history of this ancient race becomes a sort of symbolic account of the soul experiences of a people. In so doing, Philo went too far and for this reason: He did not possess the judgment and insight born of spiritual science that would have enabled him to discern and know when the descriptions concerning external events glided into portrayals relative to soul life.

As we proceed, it will be realized that in Moses we have a personality who influenced directly the active course of human evolution and whose mission it was to enlighten humankind concerning matters of the utmost import and significance. When we experience that deep sense, so pregnant with meaning, through which we become aware that his deeds still touch a chord within our souls, then do we feel that a full and clear comprehension of the Moses impulse is to us a necessity. We will, therefore, without further preamble, enter at once upon the question of his great mission. The true object of his life's work cannot be fully understood unless we presuppose that the Bible narrative was based upon actual and specific knowledge of a certain fundamental change in the human being's psychic condition, to which we have already referred when considering the individualities of Zarathustra, Hermes, and Buddha. We then drew attention to the fact that during the course of evolution the soul life of the human being has gradually undergone a definite modification, from a divine primordial clairvoyant state to that of our present-day intellectual consciousness.

I must once again bring back to your minds a statement made in previous lectures, namely, that in primeval times the soul of human beings was so constituted that during certain intermediary conditions between that of sleeping and being awake they could gaze upon the spirit world and that things thus observed, and which were truly of the spiritual realms, manifested as pictures or visions; it is these visions that in many cases have been perpetuated in the form of mythological legends of olden times. In reply to the question "How can the reality of this ancient clairvoyant consciousness be proved externally and without the aid of spiritual science?" we would say that the answer is to be found in the results of certain precise and painstaking investigations carried on even in our own time but which have not as yet received general recognition. We would point out that comparatively recently some of our mythologists, during their researches into the origin of ancient mythical visions and legends that have arisen among certain separate and distinctive peoples, have been forced to assume the existence of an altogether different conscious state in order to account for these ancient myths and concepts.

I have often referred to an interesting book, entitled *The Riddle of the Sphinx*[7] by Ludwig Laistner, a mythologist who must be ranked as the most prominent among the modern investigators in this field of research. *The Riddle of the Sphinx* is regarded as one of the most important works of its kind. Laistner draws attention to the fact that certain myths appear to form a sequel to events typical of experiences in a dream world. He did not advance so far as the study of spiritual science, and he was quite unaware that he had in reality laid the foundation stone of a true knowledge and understanding of the ancient mythologies. We cannot, however, regard myths and legends merely in the light of transfigured typical dreams, as Laistner has done; we must recognize in them the products of a former condition of human consciousness in which the human being could apprehend the spirit world in pictorial visions that later found expression in mythical imagery.

It is impossible to comprehend the old fables and legends unless we start with the hypothesis that they were evolved from a different form of conscious state; it is just because this basic assumption has been lacking that they are so little understood. This prehistoric soul state has now given way to our present intellectual consciousness, the latter of which may be briefly characterized as follows: We alternate between a condition of sleeping and of being awake. In our wakeful state we seize upon those impressions that come to us from the external world through the medium of our senses. These ideas we group together, combining them by means of our intellect. This material form of intellectual consciousness, which acts

7. *Das Rätsel der Sphinx: Grundzüge einer Mythengeschichte*, 2 vols. Berlin: Wilhelm Hertz, 1889.

through our power of understanding and intelligence, has now superseded the ancient clairvoyant soul state. We have thus characterized a particular episode of history and presented it in the aspect it assumes when we make a profound study of the evolution of humankind.

There is yet another factor underlying the manner in which Bible narratives are expressed. It appears that a special mission was assigned to each nation, race, and tribe in connection with the evolution and development of human beings and that the ancient clairvoyant forms of consciousness manifested in differ-ent ways according to the capacity and temperament of the var-ious peoples. For this reason we find fundamentally among the mythologies and pagan religions of divers nations such unifor-mity of tradition concerning this old clairvoyant state.

We thus realize that we are not dealing with just one abstract idea, or unit, in this ancient conception of the world, for the most varied missions were assigned to nations and to peoples who differed very greatly from one another. Thus it came about that the universal consciousness found expression in many and varying forms. If we would indeed understand all that the evolution of humankind implies, then we must take into consideration the fact that it does not consist merely of a meaningless succession of civilizations but that throughout the whole course of human progress and development there is found interwoven both significance and purport. Hence we find that a certain order of conscious state may reappear and be found active in some later civilization because, like a fresh page or a newborn flower, it has something to add to that which has gone before, for the whole meaning and purpose of human evolution implies ever-recurrent and successive forms of manifestation.

We can best understand the people of a nation from the perspective of spiritual science when we realize that all races, be
they ancient Indians, Persians, Babylonians, Greeks, or
Romans, had a definite mission to fulfill and that each nation
gave expression in some special and distinctive manner to that
which was active and could live in human consciousness. We
cannot rightly comprehend these different peoples unless we
are in a position to apprehend and realize the nature of their
mission from their individual characteristics. The whole evolution of humankind proceeds in such a way that to each nation
a certain time is apportioned; when this period draws to a
close, the nation's work is done. It is as if the hour had struck,
the seeds had brought forth their fruit, and the task was ended.
It may, however, happen that with this or that race certain
peculiarities of temperament or natural disposition corresponding to a former period may persist. In such a case the
particular nation has, as it were, passed over the appointed
time when a new mission should be entered upon and take the
place of that which was before. Thus it is that certain singular
and distinctive national traits may endure and become active at
a later period, at a time when the objective course of human
evolution substitutes some fresh purpose for that which was
previously determined.

A course of events of this nature is especially noticeable with
the Egyptians, and we have already become acquainted with
their peculiar characteristics during the lecture devoted to Hermes. The Egyptians had been assigned a lofty mission in connection with the collective progress and development of
humanity, and all that was embodied therein was perfected and
fulfilled while the seeds of that which was to follow had been
laid in the Egyptian civilization. The people of this great

nation, however, retained their original temperament and singular characteristics and were not of themselves capable of formulating and undertaking a new mission. It thus came about that the control and government of the succeeding community passed into other hands. The source out of which the fresh movement evolved was fundamentally Egyptian, but the mission itself was destined to assume a different character.

Here we note something akin to a change of tendency in the whole purport of human evolution; in order that we may understand the circumstances, it is necessary that we immerse ourselves deeply in the study of all that pertained to the growth and development of the Egyptian mission. When Moses had acquired all the knowledge and information possible concerning this matter, he pondered deeply, and the souls of his people were stirred. It was, however, not his task to carry on the ancient Egyptian mission; he was meant to evolve out of it some entirely new plan that he might instill into the course of human evolution. It is because his concept was so mighty, so comprehensive, and so penetrating in its nature that the personality of Moses exerted such a powerful influence upon the whole history of humankind. The way in which the Moses mission evolved out of the past evolution of the Egyptian people is even in our day of the greatest interest, and its example and study still bear abundant fruit. The knowledge and understanding that came to Moses from the Egyptians and were enhanced through his contact with the lofty and eternal course of spiritual development have reached ever outward, until they have now become active in our soul life.

The impression we have gained of Moses is that of a personality not directly dependent upon any particular period or upon any special mission for the wisdom that was his to impart

Moses

to humanity. We regard him as one whose soul must have been stirred by those eternally surging waves of divine influence that always find new channels through which to reach deep down into the evolution of humankind, so that human beings may be productive and bring forth goodly fruits. It is as if the everlasting germ of wisdom implanted in the soul of Moses found its fitting soil and ripened in the light of the knowledge that came to him from the Egyptian civilization.

The Bible account of the finding of Moses enclosed in an ark shortly after his birth (Exodus 2:5) is a symbolic description according to the ancient mode, from which we are to understand that in Moses we are concerned with a soul that drew upon eternal sources for the most lofty of those concepts that it proffered to humanity. Anyone who understands the singular form in which such religious narratives are developed knows that this particular style is always indicative of some matter of deep significance. During former lectures of this series, we have learned that when human beings desire to raise their capacity of apprehension to the higher level of the spiritual spheres, they must pass through certain stages of soul development during which they completely shut themselves off from the external world and also from that ever-wakeful call emanating from the lowest forces of the soul.

Let us suppose that we wished to express figuratively that at birth some personality entering upon earthly life came upon the world endowed with certain divine gifts that would later raise him to great heights in his relation to humankind. We might well indicate this concept by developing a narrative telling us that it was essential that this being, shortly after birth, should pass through a material experience of such a nature as to cause all his sense perceptions and powers of external apprehension to be for a time entirely shut off from the physical world.[8] Viewed in this light, the Bible story concerning the discovery of Moses becomes quite intelligible.

We read that the daughter of the Egyptian king Pharaoh [sent her maid to the river to fetch the ark in which was the child] and that she herself named him Moses—"Because," she said, "I drew him out of the water" (Exodus 2:10). Those who are aware of the true meaning of the name "Moses" know that it signifies this act, as is indicated in the Bible. From this graphic narrative we are to understand that the daughter of Pharaoh, who is here symbolic of Egyptian culture, guided the influx of external life into a soul touched with the attributes of eternity. At the same time we find intimated in a wonderful way that the imperishable message Moses was destined to bring to humanity was, one might say, enfolded and lay within an outer shell encompassed and enveloped by the old Egyptian culture and mission.

Next follow descriptions of external events that occurred during the life development of Moses, and we realize once again from the form in which they are presented that they have reference to actual outer happenings. All that we read concerning the vicissitudes of Moses, especially where mention is made of his grief and distress over the bondage of his people in Egypt, may be regarded as an actual account of mundane events. As the story continues, it merges almost imperceptibly into a graphic portrayal of his inner soul life and soul experiences. This occurs at that place where it is stated that he fled

---

8. The underlying suggestion here is that the *fact* that it is necessary for the perceptual faculties to be held in abeyance for the time being indicates that this particular personality already possessed other faculties of a spiritual order, which being thus freed would become operative.

I'm wondering if in today's time 8/2015 there are any great initiates, can't think of any that will affect humankind!

away and was finally guided to a priest of Midian whose name was Jethro or Reu'el (Exodus 2:15–20).

Anyone having the knowledge and discernment necessary to discover the existence of a story of this nature underlying what at first sight would appear to be an ordinary spiritual narrative would at once realize from the very names alone that the account changes its whole character at this point and passes over to a description of soul events. We do not mean to suggest that Moses did not actually set out upon a journey to some temple sanctuary or abode of priestly learning but rather that the whole narrative has been most ingeniously developed and told in such manner that external happenings are deliberately intermingled with the soul experiences of the great patriarch. Thus do we find that all outer life experiences mentioned at this point are suggestive of the trials and tribulations against which Moses struggled in order to attain a more exalted soul state.

What, then, is the actual significance of Jethro? From the Bible we learn that he was one of those mysterious individualities whom we meet again and again when we study the evolution and development of the human race. They are beings who stand supreme in having won their way through toil and effort to that lofty standard of knowledge and discernment which can be acquired, slowly and gradually, only through true experience of the soul's inner conflicts. It is in this way alone that human beings may gain true understanding of those grand spiritual heights where lie the paths traversed by such exalted ones. Moses became, to a certain extent, a disciple of Jethro, and through this association his mission was destined to receive a direct impulse. Now Jethro was one of those incomprehensible beings who withhold their innermost nature from the apprehension of humankind, while acting on occasion as teachers and leaders of human beings. Today there is much doubt and incredulity regarding the reality of such mystic personalities, but that they have indeed existed becomes evident to every earnest student of the historical development of humanity.

The account of the experiences of Moses while he was a disciple of this great wise priest opens with a description of his meeting with Jethro's seven daughters [in the land of Midian, Exodus 2:15, 16] near a well (a symbol betokening a source of wisdom). Anyone who would comprehend the deeper significance underlying a graphic narrative of this nature must remember above all that mystical descriptions of every period have symbolically portrayed all such knowledge and power as the soul itself may display in the form of female figures—even down to Goethe, who in the closing words of *Faust* alludes to the "eternal feminine." In the seven daughters of Jethro, then, we recognize the seven human soul forces over which that priestly character exercised control.[9]

We must bear in mind that in those ancient times when human consciousness was still enlivened by the old clairvoyance, other views prevailed regarding the nature of the human

---

9. The seven human soul forces to which reference is here made are those cosmic influences that act through the soul in connection with the seven principles of the human organism. The first four principles are as follows: the physical body, the etheric or life body, the astral body, and the "I"- or body of consciousness; the latter sets about transforming the first three by acting upon the psychic principles. Within the "I" we have the last three principles: atman, or spirit human as transmuted physical body; buddhi, or life spirit as transmuted etheric or life body; and manas, or spirit self as transmuted astral body. The latter, manas, is partly developed; of atman and buddhi there is merely a seed.

① atman or spirit human or physical body
② buddhi or life spirit or etheric
③ manas or spirit self or astral body
④ I or body consciousness

soul and its various powers. The only way in which we can form any conception of this primordial consciousness is by starting with our current ideas as a basis. We speak today of the human being's soul and its powers of thinking, feeling, and willing as if these forces were within us, contained, one might say, in the very soul itself; this concept is essentially correct as viewed from the standpoint of intellectual consciousness. Primeval human beings, under the influence of their gift for clairvoyant vision, regarded the soul and its workings from a different aspect. They were not aware of any centralized system in this connection and did not look upon their powers of thought, feeling, and will as forces whose midpoint of activity is situated in the Ego and which determine the oneness and individuality of the soul. Instead, they regarded themselves as wholly subservient to the macrocosm and its several forces, while each separate source of energy within their souls seemed to be linked with specific and divine spiritual beings. This concept may be compared to one in which we might conceive our thought activities as prompted and maintained by some spiritual soul power other than that which stimulates and influences the faculties of feeling and will. We would thus picture separate currents of spiritual energy as flowing inward from the macrocosm and activating our powers of thought, feeling, and willing. Although in these days we form no such conception, it was thus that primeval human beings regarded the soul—not as a centralized unit in itself but rather as a stage upon which the divine spiritual powers of the cosmos might unceasingly play their several parts. In connection with Moses, reference is made to seven such forces conceived as active upon the stage of soul life.

We have only to turn to Plato to realize that the human being's outlook on the evolution of human consciousness changed and became in general more and more abstract and intellectual. Plato conceived "Ideas" to be living entities, leading an existence such as in our time could be thought of only in connection with matter; each separate soul force is pictured as possessing an attribute that plays its part in the theater of the soul's totality. Gradually, the conceptions formed regarding the capacity of the soul became increasingly abstract while the unity of the Ego assumed more and more its rightful place in human beings' concepts. Strange as it may appear, in the medieval conception of the seven liberal arts we can still distinguish in abstract form characteristics typical of the symbolic representation of the seven active spiritual forces of soul life in the seven daughters of the Midianite priest Jethro.[10] The manner in which the seven liberal arts evolved and were brought to light was as a last dim echo (touched with a modern trend of thought) of the consciousness that recognized that seven distinct faculties persist and remain active in the scenes staged in the theater of the human soul.

When we consider these concepts, we begin to realize that while, from the spiritual standpoint, Moses was confronted with the collective aspect of these seven human soul forces, his chief mission was nevertheless to implant one particular soul influence in the form of an impulse deeply and fully into the course of human evolution. It was possible for him to do so

10. In the Middle Ages, the Liberal Arts (*arte liberales*) were considered to be seven in number, namely, music, grammar, rhetoric, logic, arithmetic, geometry, and astronomy. Plato and Aristotle distinguished between the practical arts and the so-called liberal arts, of which the latter were concerned with progress of an ethical or literary character.

because it lay in the blood and in the temperament of his people to manifest a special interest in that outstanding soul
power, the activities of which have been felt down to our own
time and which it was his task to instill. We refer to that dominant soul energy that unites all those forces previously
regarded as separate and detached into one centralized and
homogeneous bond of inner soul life—the life of the true self,
the Ego. We are next told that one of the daughters of Jethro
married Moses; this means that within his soul one of these
forces became specially active, so much so that owing to its
influence it became for a long period a dominating power in
human evolution, reducing all other soul forces to a unified
soul-Ego.

Statements such as these must be made with the greatest
reserve, for in our present age humankind has no adequate faculty or organ with which they may realize that many biblical
descriptions that apparently represent external happenings are
presented solely for the purpose of drawing attention to the
fact that at the time at which the events portrayed took place a
particular soul was undergoing some experience of inner development. In other words, the soul was especially concerned
with and attracted to its individual mission. It is also apparent
that one special attribute the old Egyptians did not possess—
the inspiration that Moses drew from the human Ego-force at
the midpoint of the human being's soul powers—was for him
the criterion [to which he referred his judgment].

We can therefore with reason assert that the true mission of
the ancient Egyptian nation was to found a culture based upon
the practice and methods of primeval clairvoyance. All that is
best of those things handed down to us from the Egyptian civilization has sprung from the singular nature of those peculiar

psychic powers once possessed by the Egyptian priests and the leaders of the people. But the time came when with respect to the old Egyptian mission the cosmic clock had run down and the call had to go forth to humankind to unfold and develop those soul forces that it was ordained should, for a long period of time, supersede that ancient passive clairvoyant condition in the future evolution of humanity.

Ego-consciousness, intellectuality, rationalism, reason, and understanding, with their spheres of action in the external perceptual world, were destined to replace the old clairvoyant consciousness in the human race yet to come. I have already stated how, in the future of humankind, clairvoyant power and intellectual consciousness will be united. Even now humanity is advancing toward a time when these two conscious states will be universally interwoven and co-active throughout the human race. The most important element in human culture, regarded from our modern standpoint, received its first impulse through Moses; thus we have a sense of persistency in connection with the Moses impulse that still exists in our soul life and power. To Moses was granted a certain capacity for intellectual thought and action controlled by *reason* and *understanding*. This ability [and his wisdom] were instilled into him in a singular and unusual manner, because all those concepts and ideas that came to him and were destined to manifest and bear fruit in some particular way at a later period must first have been implanted in a fashion conforming with the peculiar methods in vogue in those ancient times. Here we come upon a remarkable fact, namely, that later generations of humankind were directly indebted to Moses for their power of expanding and developing their understanding and intellect through the medium of their Ego-consciousness so that they might reason and ponder upon the world and gain enlightenment through inner intellectual contemplation while yet fully awake.

The manner in which a consciousness of intellectuality came to Moses must have been through flashes of intellectual awareness similar in nature to the old clairvoyant manifestations. He was indeed the recipient of that first initial impulse toward the new order of reasoned judgment and understanding while at the same time he possessed the old clairvoyant power, being in fact under the influence of the last of its promptings. All the knowledge and enlightenment that was acquired by later generations independently of clairvoyance was accessible to Moses through its aid. His understanding, discernment, and intuition in the sphere of pure reason came to him when his soul passed into that same clairvoyant condition which he had experienced when under the influence of the old Midianite priest. We have the incident of the burning bush, which glowed with fire of such a nature that it was not consumed. In this case, the spirit of the cosmos manifested before Moses in an entirely new manner, beyond the clairvoyant knowledge of the Egyptians to explain.

Everyone who is acquainted with the essential facts knows that during the course of development the human soul reaches a point when the aspect of external objects gradually undergoes a change, so that they appear interwoven with that mysterious background of archetypes from which they emanate. The spectacle of the "burning bush" so magnificently portrayed in the Bible is recognized by all who are advanced in spiritual discernment as an instance of human apprehension of the spirit world. We now realize that the enlightenment Moses received in clairvoyant form must have been of the nature of a new consciousness proceeding from the great spirit of the cosmos, the spirit that is ever active and weaves throughout the whole material world. Ancient peoples believed in a *plurality* of cosmic forces, and they conceived these forces as operating in the human soul in such a way that the soul's power did not represent a unit, for the forces were manifold in nature while the soul was regarded merely as the scene of their active expression. It was for Moses to recognize a cosmic spirit of a very different order—one that did not manifest as a soul power, owing its origin to various spirit influences that while exhibiting a certain similitude find ultimate expression in varied form. The spirit of the cosmos, which it was ordained that Moses should apprehend, was of a wholly different character, for its revelation can alone take place in the innermost and holiest midpoint of soul life, the Ego. There works the spirit of the universe—in the place where the human soul is conscious of its very center.

When the human soul feels that the Ego is linked with the weaving and the life of the spirit, in the same way as the people of old realized that their being was truly related to the cosmic forces, then can it apprehend those things first revealed to Moses through his clairvoyant powers. These revelations must be regarded as forming the cosmic basis from which came the great impulse he gave to humankind—that primal impulse enabling humanity through its reasoning faculties and understanding alone [unaided by the old clairvoyance] to associate and compare physical phenomena and to recognize in them factors underlying all continuity in the material world.

If we consider the center of our soul life today, it appears to be of extremely poor content, despite the fact that this content represents our most intense life experiences. Certain people, especially those of a highly gifted and talented character, as for instance, Jean Paul,[11] have felt sometime during the course of earthly existence that they were actually confronted with their true center of being. In his autobiography Jean Paul tells this story:

> Never shall I forget an inner vision that I once experienced and which I have not as yet described to anyone. In this vision I was present at the birth of my true conscious self, and I clearly recollect both the time and the place of this occurrence. It was one morning when I was a very young child; I was standing in the doorway of our house, and as I looked toward the left, in the direction of the woodshed, there suddenly came to me an inner vision flashed down as lightning from Heaven of the words:—"I AM AN I" [Ich bin ein Ich]—and these words remained for a space shining brightly. In that moment and in that place, my "I" had looked upon itself for the first time, and the gaze would endure forever. Illusion due to defect of memory is hardly conceivable in this case, since no outside incidents or topics could mingle extraneous matter with an event that could take place only in the secret and most holy seclusion of the human being's innermost being and the very novelty of which caused minor details to be deeply impressed upon my memory.

This "secret and most holy seclusion" appears to be the most intense and powerful condition of our soul life, but human

---

11. Jean Paul (1763–1825), born Johann Paul Friedrich Richter, was a popular German writer whose novels and stories were welcomed by a wide circle of admirers during his lifetime.

beings cannot be so aware of this particular soul state as of many another, for it is lacking in [conscious] plentitude. When human beings withdraw themselves to this central point, then do they indeed realize that through those wondrous words "I AM"—so earnest and forceful but at the same time so meager in actual word content—there ever resounds the dominant tone of their innermost soul being.

That spirit from the cosmos, which Moses clearly apprehended as a homogeneous unity, is unceasingly active in that abode of "secret and most holy seclusion." No wonder that when this cosmic essence was first revealed to Moses he cried out, "If I am appointed to the task of standing before the people in order to inaugurate a new civilization based upon the consciousness of self, who will believe me? In *whose name* shall I proclaim my mission?" And the answer came: "Thou shalt say 'I AM THAT I AM.'" This profound declaration signifies that the name of the divinity who reveals himself in the "secret and most holy seclusion" of human nature cannot be otherwise proclaimed than with words that designate the consciousness of self-being. In the phenomenon of the burning bush, Moses discerned the Yahweh, or Jehovah nature, and we can well understand that from the moment when the name yahweh broke in upon his consciousness as "I AM" there came a new current, a new element into the course of human evolution that was destined from that time on to supplant the old Egyptian civilization. The ancient culture had merely served to develop the soul of Moses in order that he might be in a position to truly appreciate and cope with those most exalted personalities and difficult situations that it would be his lot to encounter during the course of his life experiences.

Up to that cosmic hour the Egyptians had had a mission to fulfill based upon the powers of a bygone clairvoyant conscious state, but the time allotted to that mission had passed. Henceforth, the race, if it should continue to live on, would remain endowed with the same temperament and national characteristics it had heretofore possessed. It had found no means whereby it might raise itself and cross the boundary that separated the old epoch from the new. But at this very time it was ordained that the Hebrew people would arise and that Moses should point out a way. In remembrance of the events connected with the "passing over" by Moses and his people from that period that was ended to that which was to come, there has ever since been celebrated the feast of the Passover; this festival should constantly remind us that it was *Moses* who was blessed with the understanding and the wisdom that made possible the transition from the old order of consciousness to the new. The Egyptians could not span this gulf, and as the nation tarried the waves of time swept onward. It is in the manner outlined here that we must regard the relationship of Moses to the Egyptians and to his people.

We next come to the conference between Moses and Pharaoh. It is easy to see that when these two came together, they could not understand each other. The account is intended to convey the idea that all those things about which Moses spoke proceeded from an entirely changed order of human consciousness and must, therefore, have been quite unintelligible to Pharaoh, in whom only the old clairvoyant Egyptian culture continued to be active. That such was the case is evident from the way in which the records are expressed, for Moses spoke a new language. He clothed his speech in words that emanated from the Ego-consciousness of the human soul and were therefore incomprehensible to Pharaoh, who could follow only the old train of thought.

The Hebrew race was by nature thoroughly adapted to receive the great enlightenment that it was the mission of Moses to impart. What was its actual character? It was ordained that the old clairvoyant state should give place to an intellectual reasoning consciousness. It has been pointed out in previous lectures that clairvoyant consciousness is in no way connected with our external corporeal nature and that it unfolds freely just at those times when human beings, through their soul training, have released themselves from their external bodily instrument so that they may be active and untrammeled in their soul life. The intellectual consciousness is associated with the brain and the blood, and its means of expression lies in the human organism.

The continued spiritual development of the conscious state that had previously hovered over the physical structure had, up to the time of Moses, been brought about solely through the relationship existing between master and pupil, but it had now to accommodate itself to a new condition in which it would be directly connected with and confined to the physical organism and to the blood that would flow in the veins of the people from generation to generation. It was for this reason that the enlightenment Moses was destined to give to humanity, so as to bring about an impulse toward an intellectual culture, could be instilled only into a nation in which the blood of the race would continue to flow vigorously throughout future generations, and therefore of such a nature was the instrument chosen to receive the basal principles of the new cognitive faculty.

The new reasoning consciousness, the seeds of which were implanted by Moses, was not destined to live on merely in the spirit, for it had been ordained that the people thus chosen should be taken away from the Egyptian nation in the midst of which they had been made ready and that from that time onward, isolated and as a separate race, they must develop through centuries those external methods and means that would in future form the basis of an intellectual culture, which should continue throughout all coming ages.

We thus realize that the world's history is full of significance and purport and that the spiritual element is closely related to all external physical agents. It is clear that the author of the Bible narrative is at great pains to present the account of the transition of the ancient Egyptian culture to that of Moses in its true light and meaning as an episode in the history of the world. We have, for instance, the story of the passing of the children of Israel through the Red Sea. Concealed beneath this narrative lies a wonderful truth relative to the evolution of humankind but which is to be understood only by those who clearly comprehend the whole nature of this incident.

In connection with the Egyptians, we find proof of the link that necessarily exists between the soul powers and the clairvoyant faculty. We obtain the clearest insight into this matter when we take the animal organism as our starting point, but I am sure you will not assume that by so doing I would suggest that human nature resembles that of the animal kingdom. We must first imagine that the whole outlook and soul life of brute creation are dreamy and torpid compared with the intellectual soul state of human beings. Although primeval human clairvoyance most certainly cannot be directly compared with the soul life of animals, from which it differs radically, we can nevertheless clearly trace a definite relationship between the instinctive existence and soul life of brute creation and that of the ancient soul

life of human beings. Although it is often exaggerated, there is a
certain amount of truth underlying those stories that tell of animals leaving districts subject to earthquakes and volcanic dis-
turbances days before an eruption takes place. It has certainly
happened, in some cases, that while human beings, who regard
and apprehend all things through the medium of their intellect,
have remained unmoved, the animals in the neighborhood have
been aroused. Anyone who has a knowledge of spiritual science
knows that brute nature is so closely interwoven with all life in
its immediate environment that we can, in a sense, assert that
animals possess a measure of instinctive understanding, which
through its rudimentary powers controls and regulates their
existence. This faculty is no longer found in human beings,
because they have developed a higher intellectual quality
through which they are able to form reasoned concepts and
ideas concerning all things that come within their cognizance.
But this very logical capacity has, in effect, torn asunder that
close tie with nature they once enjoyed.

We must picture that in primeval times human beings
possessed similar instinctive cognition, both in connection
with the old clairvoyant state and also with their relationship
to the external phenomena of nature—a kind of intuition
whereby the ancients could say, "Such and such events are
about to occur, and for this reason we must take certain steps
to prepare ourselves in advance." Just in the same way some
people who are suitably constituted raise themselves through
striving of soul to a higher power of discernment and attain to
an order of apprehension concerning matters connected with
nature for which no cause or reason can be assigned.

Those who use the forces of their soul and through its
attributes and its virtues win power to utter statements beyond

the scope of their intellectual consciousness feel uncomfortable when people come to them and say, "Why is that so? Give us proof of your assertions." Such persons never realize that knowledge of this nature comes by quite a different path from that born of logical reasoning. It is a striking and pertinent fact that Goethe, when he looked out a window, could often predict hours in advance what kind of weather was in store. If we conceive faculties of this nature as existing among the ancients and manifesting in such a way that through direct contact with the spirit world the people of old were able to be closely associated with creation and the phenomena of nature (but in a manner entirely different from that which is the case today), then we can realize and picture at least one fundamental feature of the old clairvoyance relative to the practical conduct of life. In olden times humanity did not possess meteorological observatories, and there were no weather forecasts published in newspapers or in other ways, as there are today. But the ancients were endowed with a sense of perception that clearly foretold what would occur, and they governed their actions in accordance with the impressions received.

This was especially the case with the old Egyptians, among whom the faculty of sense perception was developed to a very high degree. They had no knowledge of our modern science or our analytical methods, but nonetheless they knew how to comport themselves so as to be in living harmony with the whole surrounding world. Because the cosmic hour had struck for the Egyptian culture, however, this faculty, once so prominent, fell into decadence, and the Egyptian people became less and less capable of understanding and dealing with the facts and realities of nature and could no longer foretell from the grouping and interaction of external elements and factors what should be their attitude and mode of conduct. Humanity was now destined to learn how to investigate and to study the arrangement and interrelations of these external elements; it was Moses who would impart the impulse, but the impulse that he gave came even then from his old clairvoyant consciousness.

While Moses and his people stood upon the shore of the Red Sea, he realized, through an understanding somewhat similar to our own but which still unfolded clairvoyantly, that exceptional natural circumstances, namely, an unusual combination of an East Wind and ebb tide together with a channel-like passage, made it possible at the right moment for him to lead the Israelites across shallow waters. This historical fact has been graphically portrayed so that we may realize that Moses was indeed the founder of a new and universal mode of intellectual apprehension that is still active in our day and through which humanity will once more learn to bring the practical affairs of life into harmony with the existing order of nature, even as was done by that great patriarch.

The Egyptians were a nation whose hour was spent; they could no longer foretell what would come to pass. The power of the old instinctive faculties that were theirs in long-ago times had waned, and they found themselves once more in a position, as in the past, when a decision must be made. In olden times they would have cried out, "It is too late. We cannot now make the passage." But that innate gift of discernment they had so long enjoyed had all but vanished, and they knew not how to live in the new intellectual conscious state. Therefore they stood before the Red Sea, helpless and bewildered. The old clairvoyant consciousness could no longer be their guide; [they followed,] and disaster overtook them. Here we find the new Moses element in direct contrast with the old, and we see that the ancient clairvoyant faculty had so far declined that it could no longer be relied upon; because it was unsuited to the new age, it was the forerunner of calamity.

When we look beneath the surface of such apparently external graphic narratives as this and come upon the matter the narrator really has in mind, we find that the stories often characterize great turning points in the evolution of humankind. We realize that it is no light task to deduce from the peculiar descriptions found in the ancient writings the true significance of the various personalities mentioned, such as, for instance, Moses in the circumstances we have just quoted. It is clear from what follows later in the account that at that time, when it had to be decided whether Moses should or should not lead his people to Palestine, he still relied entirely upon the old clairvoyance; in his case his intellectual enlightenment was fundamentally dependent upon this faculty. It was because the blood that flowed in the veins of the Jewish people made them by nature especially suitable to the task of laying the foundation of the impending movement toward intellectuality that it was ordained they should be led forth and guided to the Promised Land. The knowledge and wisdom Moses acquired through his clairvoyant powers sufficed to impart the necessary impulse but could not itself be of the new culture, for this new cultural faculty was destined to manifest in ways that would be the antithesis of the old order of clairvoyant consciousness.

From the Bible account it is evident that Moses felt that his call was merely to lead his people to a certain place. He was not to take them into the Promised Land; the last stage of the journey must be left to those who were destined to embrace the new order of intellectual development. Although Moses was the prophet of the Lord, who manifests in our very Ego- being, we are nevertheless given to understand that it was only by virtue of his clairvoyant faculty that he could become conscious of the mighty word of the great spirit of the cosmos. When at last he was left to himself with the task of aiding his people, he fled to his tent so that through his clairvoyant powers he might once more be in the actual presence of his God. Then it was that a voice said, "Because thou canst not carry out all that is betokened by those thoughts that come to thee with visions, henceforth must another be the leader of thy people." The words of this decree shed a radiance around the great patriarch, for they implied that Moses, with his clairvoyant faculty, was a prophet the like of whom would no more be seen in Israel. We are to understand that Moses was the last among the ancients to be endowed with the old order of psychic discernment. From that time on would a form of intellection wholly independent of this gift spread its influence among all peoples fitted to the task and the human being's actions and cognition be based on the power to reason and tradition alone. Thus might the Ego, the truth of which had already been recognized by those who had understanding of the fundamental factors of the new culture, be made ready that it might absorb a new principle.

It was through the mission of Moses that humankind was first led to realize that the most positive feeling human beings can experience of the absolute reality of the all-pervading cosmic spirit, that divine principle that is ever active and interwoven throughout the whole earth, is centered in the "I AM"—the very midpoint of the human soul. But in order that these two simple words might be imbued with the utmost import, the "I AM" must first store within itself the full measure of a content that will once again embrace the world. To reach this end necessitated yet another mission, which is expressed in those deeply significant words of Saint Paul "Yet not I, but Christ liveth in me." Moses had brought humanity up to the point of establishing a true culture of the human Ego. This newborn intellect was destined to live on throughout the future ages, a gift from above, a form of civilization, a "receptacle" for the coming content. It was essential that the center of our being should first unfold in the bosom of the ancient Hebrew people. From that time onward would this divine receptacle be filled with all that springs from a true understanding of the Mystery of Golgotha and the events that took place in Palestine. Thus would the Ego receive its new content, which itself would be a creation of the spirit world. We can most easily recognize all that came of that fresh inpouring and that owed its origin to the preparation and development of the Hebrew people when we refer to the book of Job. We cannot, however, rightly understand the wonderful tragedy portrayed there unless we take into account the peculiar characteristics of the Jewish race.

We are told that Job—though he was a righteous man who believed in his God—was convinced that the Almighty was actually the true source of all his afflictions. He experienced disaster after disaster to his property, his family, and his own person. The Lord appeared to manifest in such a manner that Job might well have doubted whether indeed the great spirit of the cosmos was really active in the human Ego. Matters went to such a length that Job's wife could not understand why her husband, despite all that had befallen him, should continue to trust in the Almighty. She therefore spoke to him in words of paramount import: "Dost thou still retain thine integrity? Curse God, and die" (Job 2:9). What is the underlying meaning of this significant allegorical tragedy and of the words "curse God, and die"? It is here implied that if the God whom you regard as being the very source of your existence visits you with sorrow and adversity, you may turn from him. But death will indeed be the lot of the one who would do this thing, for he who turns away from his God places himself outside the pale of the living course of evolution. The friends of Job could not believe that he had committed no transgression, for surely in the case of a righteous person equity should prevail. Even the narrator himself cannot make clear to us the justness of the circumstances, for he can say only that Job, who was thus stricken with misery and distress, nevertheless received compensation in the physical world for all that he had lost and suffered.

Throughout this deeply significant allegory depicted in the book of Job there is an echo of the Moses consciousness. In the story it is made clear that the spirit brings to us enlightenment and ever manifests in the human being's innermost being. But during the course of earthly existence the Ego must live in contact with physical things. Thus it is that there are moments of transgression in which human beings may weaken and lose their feeling of unity with the vital source of life. From the Christ impulse, humanity has learned that compensation for suffering and affliction is not to be sought in the physical world alone. We now know that in every case when human beings are overcome by bodily distress—in sorrow and in pain—if they remain steadfast, they may indeed triumph over that which is material. For the Ego is not merely illumined by the ultimate source of all that is spread throughout space and time but is so conditioned that it may yet absorb the mighty power of the eternal.

We find the same uplifting thoughts underlying Saint Paul's words "Yet not I, but Christ liveth in me." Moses had brought humanity so far that it could realize that all things that live and weave throughout the cosmos manifest in deepest and most characteristic form in the Ego. Human beings may comprehend the world if it is pictured as a simple unit proceeding from some great universal Ego center. If we would indeed receive the eternal spirit within our being, then must we not regard merely temporal things or take heed only of the Jehovah-Unit hidden and beyond all that is of space and time, but must we look also to that spontaneous and glorious benefaction—the Christ source—which underlies and is concentric with all unity.

Thus do we recognize in Moses the personality of one who paved the way for Christianity. We have learned in what manner he instilled into humanity a consciousness of self, a consciousness that throughout the development of all future generations would be a storehouse to be filled with the substance of eternity, which means that it was yet to become a fitting receptacle replete with the essence of the Christ-being. It is in this way that we picture the patriarch Moses in his relation to the progress and evolution of humanity. History always reveals its deepest truths when subject to thought and reflection of this nature.

In a previous lecture devoted to Buddha we drew attention to the fact that from time to time some outstanding personality arises, through whose agency the eternal fount of wisdom springs once more to life, causing humanity to advance yet another step in its growth and development. When we ponder the circumstances connected with this or that great figure, there comes to us a sense of his true relation to the collective evolution of humanity. When we regard the development of the human race from this perspective, we find that we are

involved in its progress in a vital sense; it is at once apparent
that the spirits of the cosmos have some fixed and definite purpose associated with our existence, the object of which
becomes more and more discernible as life proceeds. It is
through the earnest consideration of the example and works of
lofty spiritual individualities, together with profound meditation concerning outstanding events in the world's evolution
and the history of humankind, that we may gain that sense of
power, confidence of soul, and unswerving hope through which
alone we may take our proper place in the totality of human
evolution. If we regard the history of the world in this manner,
we feel anew the beauty of Goethe's words, and we realize that
the greatest benefit that can accrue to us through the study of
universal history is the awakening of our enthusiasm. But it
must be an enthusiasm that is not mere blind admiration and
wonder, for it should prompt us to implant in our souls the
seeds borne to us from the past, so that they may bring forth
goodly fruits in the time yet to come.

The words of the great poet live again, in somewhat modified form, when through the contemplation of those grand
outstanding personalities and events of olden times we realize
this glorious truth:

The age is as a field in flower,
Where wondrous growth and life proceed;
Fresh buds unfold with every hour—
Lo! all is fruit and all is seed.[12]

---

12. Die Zeit, sie ist eine blühende Flur,
    Ein grosses Lebendiges ist der Menschheit Werdegang,
    Und alles ist Frucht und alles ist Same!

5. ELIJAH

THE PROPHET ELIJAH shines forth as one of the most resplendent stars in the firmament of human spiritual evolution, and the great illumination he brought to humanity in olden times has endured even to the present day. The deeds, the characteristics, the greatness of this outstanding personality as portrayed in the ancient biblical records make the profoundest impression upon the hearts and feelings of humanity; nevertheless, this significant figure seems difficult to comprehend with respect to external history. We are about to consider Elijah from the standpoint of spiritual science. Viewed in its light, we find in the very nature of his being an indication that the most important causes and motives underlying the circumstances connected with earthly existence during human evolution are not dependent merely upon those ideas that may be consciously apprehended and the results of which can be recognized externally as forming a part of life's history. For we learn that those very impulses that move us to actions of greatest import are born within the confines of the soul.

In order that this truth, which sheds so great a light upon the world's history, may become apparent to our spiritual vision, we need only recall the fact that Christianity owes its foundation, for the most part, to that profound psychic incident experienced by Saint Paul [Saul], which found outward expression in the vision near Damascus (Acts 9:3). No matter how much we may argue concerning the reality and nature of this external happening, it cannot be denied that the true origin of Christianity is intimately connected with what then took place in the soul and spirit of that great apostle and righteous founder of the Christian faith and that the knowledge and enlightenment which came to him was passed on to humankind through the medium of his flaming words and self-sacrificing deeds. In many other cases it can be proved that primary causes and impulses underlying events that happen during the historical unfoldment of human existence cannot be identified with normal external occurrences, for their inception may often be traced to the hearts and souls of humanity.

We are now about to consider an example of this very nature in connection with the personality of Elijah and the period in which he lived. Since my lecture must of necessity be both brief and sketchy in character, though treating of a subject covering so wide a field, the question as to how far the matter presented will elucidate and provide new evidence concerning the progress of human historical evolution in this special instance must be left for your further consideration, but your thoughts should at all times be guided by the deep promptings of the soul. The object of my discourse is not merely to supply information concerning the personality and significance of the prophet Elijah; its true purport is at the same time to present an *example* of the manner in which spiritual science weighs and regards such matters and, by virtue of the means at its disposal, can shed fresh light upon facts connected with the growth and development of humanity, which have come to our knowledge through other sources.

With this end in view, we will employ a special method in dealing with our subject. In the first place, statements that are the result of the investigations of spiritual science and have reference to the personality and significance of Elijah will be as independent as possible of all connection with the Bible as a source, and such references will be made only when they seem essential in connection with names and descriptions. We will therefore first endeavor to portray all pertinent events as they actually happened and later draw attention to the manner in which they are depicted in the ancient biblical records. The occurrences will be set forth just as they are revealed by the researches of spiritual science, which researches have formed the basis of the various portrayals presented both in the lectures of this series and in others of previous years. A large number of my audience who, through long years of experience with the methods of spiritual science, have gained confidence in its power and proved substantiality will accept from the very first all that I propose to bring forward and regard it as trustworthy and as the result of conscientious investigation. This will be the case, even though my subject must of necessity be treated in a somewhat sketchy manner, because an exposition involving detailed proofs would require many hours for its complete presentation. To those of my audience who have had no such experience as I have mentioned, I would suggest that they look upon all that is said concerning the authentic historical narrative that I am about to unfold as if it were in the nature of a hypothesis, underlying which is a substratum of positive evidence. I am certain that if they will but do this and make a reasonable and understanding attempt, in moderation and without prejudice, to obtain the required evidence, all my statements will ultimately receive entire confirmation.

What now has spiritual science to say concerning the personality and significance of the prophet Elijah and his period? To understand this, we must go back in thought to those ancient Hebrew times when the brilliant epoch that marked the reign of Solomon was passed and the kingdom of Palestine was enduring many and varied forms of privation. We must recall the troubles of the Philistines and other similar incidents and transport ourselves in mind to those days when all that formerly constituted a united and centralized monarchy was divided into the separate kingdoms of Judah and Israel and King Ahab, who was the son of Omri, reigned in Samaria. Here we have found an opportunity to introduce biblical names, but we have done so merely for the sake of clarity and corroboration, as will often be the case as we proceed. Between King Ahab, or rather between his father and the king of Tyre and Sidon, there was a close friendship. A sort of alliance had been formed; this compact was further strengthened by the marriage of Ahab with Jezebel, a daughter of the royal house. I am making use of these names as they are familiar to us from the Bible and so that my subject may be more easily understood. We are looking back into an age when that ancient clairvoyant gift that was in general a spiritual attribute of the human being in primeval times had by no means entirely disappeared among those people who had still retained the necessary and fitting disposition. Now Queen Jezebel was endowed with this gift, and her clairvoyant powers were of a very special order; these powers, however, she did not always employ in ways destined to promote that which was good and noble. While we look upon Jezebel as a kind of clair-voyant, we must regard King Ahab as a man who only under exceptional circumstances evinced a faculty through which the hidden forces of his soul could break in upon his conscious state. In olden times such manifestations were much more in evidence and more widely spread than is the case today. There were occasions when Ahab himself experienced visions and presentiments but never to any marked extent, and they occurred only when he was confronted with some special matter connected with human destiny.

At the time to which I refer a rumor had spread throughout the land that a remarkable spirit was abroad. In reality, this was none other than he who in the Bible records bears the name of Elijah. There were few among those living in the outer world who knew precisely in what place the personality that bore this name might be found—nor did they know in what way or by what means he exerted so powerful an influence upon contemporaneous people and events. We can perhaps best describe the situation by saying that throughout the widest circles any reference to this mysterious being or even the mention of his name was accompanied by a thrill of awe; because of this it was generally felt that this spirit must possess some singular and hidden attribute of greatest import. But no one knew rightly or had indeed any idea in what way this unusual quality might manifest or where it might be sought. Only certain isolated persons, whom we might term initiates, had true knowledge of what was really taking place, and they alone knew where in the physical world they might find the outer reality of the actual individual who was the bearer of this mysterious spirit.

King Ahab was also ignorant concerning these matters, but nevertheless he experienced a peculiar feeling of apprehension, and a kind of dread overcame him whenever mention was made of that incomprehensible being regarding whom the most extravagant notions prevailed, as was only natural under the circumstances. Ahab was that king of Samaria who, through his alliance with Tyre and Sidon, had introduced into the ancient kingdom of Palestine a certain religious order that held to outer forms and ceremonies and found expression through external symbolism—in other words, a species of heathenism. Such information concerning the individuality of Elijah as came to the followers of this pagan form of worship must have created in them a strange and peculiar feeling of fear and dismay. For it was evident from what they heard that the Jahveh religion, as it may be termed, had now indeed come down to them from bygone days of the ancient Hebrew people and was once more active.

There was still a belief in one God—in one great spiritual being in the cosmos who rules over the superperceptual realm and who, by means of its forces, makes his influence felt and affects both the evolution and the history of humanity. It was further realized that the time was approaching when there would be an ever-greater and more significant understanding of Jahveh among those who were the most advanced and perfect of the descendants of the old Hebrew race. It was well known that in truth the religion of Moses contained the germ of all that one might term the Yahweh religion, but this fact had been grasped by the nation in a manner more or less after the fashion of a people yet in a stage of childhood or early youth.

The old faith, with its upturned vision toward a supersensible God, may be described only in this way: It can be likened to nothing else than to an awareness of contact with that which is invisible and superperceptual, which comes to humans when they indeed apprehend and realize their own true Ego. It was this consciousness of the supersensible that had descended upon the people. But the concept they had formed, as far as they could form any concept at all, was based upon an attempt to picture to themselves the workings of Yahweh as conceived from their experiences of the external phenomena of life. In those days it was the custom to say that Yahweh acted with regard to humanity in such a manner that when all nature was luxuriant and fruitful it was a sign that he was rewarding humanity and showering benefits upon the nation. On the other hand, when the people suffered from want and distress brought about by war, scarcity of food, and other causes, they cried out that Jehovah had turned his face away and was consumed with anger.

At that time about which we are speaking, the nation was enduring the miseries caused by a period of death and starvation; many turned aside from the god Yahweh because they could no longer believe in his works when they saw how he treated humanity, for there was a terrible famine in the land. If, indeed, we can speak of *progress* in connection with the Yahweh conception, then the progress destined to be made by these ancient Hebrew people can be characterized in the following manner: The nation must henceforth form a new Yahweh concept embodying the old thoughts and ideas, through which must flow a fuller and a higher order of human understanding so that all might say that no matter what shall take place in the outer world, whether we live in happiness or are beset with sorrows and privations, we must realize that such external events are in no way evidence of either the wrath or the benevolence of Yahweh. True devotion to God and a proper comprehension of the Yahweh concept implies that humankind will at all times gaze upward unswervingly toward the invisible deity, uninfluenced by the contemplation of outer happenings and things or the apparent reality of material impressions. Even though we meet with the direst want and affliction, through those inner forces alone that dominate the soul human beings shall come to the sure conviction that HE IS.

This great revolution in religious outlook was destined to be consummated and wrought through the power of the prophet Elijah [and, as will be seen later, his spiritual force operated at times through the medium of a chosen human personality]. When it is ordained that some great momentous change shall be brought about in the concepts of humanity, as was the case in Elijah's day, it is necessary in the beginning that there be certain fitting personalities at hand in whose souls can be implanted the germ, so to speak, of those things ordained later to enter into the history of humanity. The manner in which the seed thus laid finds fitting expression is always that of a new impulse and a new force.

If you will not misunderstand my meaning, I would say that it was decreed in accordance with the preordained fate of the nation that the individuality known as the prophet Elijah should be the chosen one whose soul should first grasp the Jehovah concept in the form I have described. To this end, it was essential that certain singular and very special forces be called up from the hidden depths of his soul—deep-seated powers as yet unknown to humankind and unguessed at even by the teachers of that time. Something in the nature of a holy mystical initiation of the highest order, through which might come the revelation of such a God, had first to take place in the innermost being of Elijah. It is therefore of the utmost importance, in order to describe in characteristic manner the way in which the Yahweh concept was instilled in the minds of the people, that we should gaze into the soul of that particular human personality in whom the spirit that was to impart the primary impulse was incarnated, or embodied—that man who, through the nature of his divine initiation, became imbued with all the latent forces of his soul. These were forces vital to one who would strike the first deep fundamental note that would call forth and make possible the coming Yahweh conception.

Such [great spiritual] personalities [as Elijah,] who are chosen to experience within the soul the first stimulating impress of some momentous forward impulse, stand for the most part isolated and alone. In olden days, however, there gathered around them certain followers who came from the great religious schools, or schools of the prophets as they were called in Palestine and which by other nations have been termed Initiation or Mystery sanctuaries. Thus we find the prophet Elijah, if we would use this name, also surrounded by a few earnest disciples who looked up to him in reverence as one exalted far above them. These disciples realized to some extent the true nature and significance of Elijah's mission, even though, because of their limited spiritual vision, they were unable to penetrate deeply into the soul of their great master. [At that time strange events had begun to take place in the land;] the people, however, had no idea where the mysterious personality might be found who had brought them about. They could say only, "He must be here or there—for something unusual is happening."

Hence it was that there spread abroad what we might term a sort of rumor (if the word is not misused) to the effect that HE, a prophet, was actually at work, but no one knew rightly where. This uncertainty was due to the exercise of a definite and peculiar influence that could be exerted by all such advanced spiritual beings as are found among outstanding

seers. Viewed in the light of our modern times, it is probable
that such a statement appears somewhat grotesque, but those
who are acquainted with the singular characteristics of that
long-ago age will find it in no way fanciful or extravagant.

All truly exalted spiritual personalities such as Elijah were
endowed with this specific and highly penetrative quality,
which made itself felt now here and now there. The activity of
this potent influence manifested in feelings of awe and dread,
and there was also a direct positive action through which it
entered little by little into the souls of the people. It there
operated in such manner as to cause them to be unable to tell,
at times, just where the external form of some great spiritual
personality might be found. But the true followers and disciples of Elijah knew well where to seek him and were further
quite aware that his outer individuality might perchance
assume a wholly unpretentious character and come to light in
connection with some quite lowly station in earthly life.

It is remarkable that at the time about which I am speaking,
the actual bearer of the spirit of Elijah was a close neighbor of
Ahab, king of Samaria, and the possessor of a small property
in his immediate vicinity, but Ahab had no suspicion that such
was the case. He sought everywhere for this singular being
whose presence was felt so mysteriously throughout the community and whom he regarded with feelings of awe and wonder, even as did his people. He entirely failed, however, to take
into consideration the simple and unassuming landowner who
lived so near him and gave no thought as to why he should, at
times, absent himself nor where he went on these occasions.
But Jezebel [being clairvoyant] had discovered that this unob-
trusive personality had actually become the external physical
embodiment of the spirit of Elijah. The knowledge she had

thus acquired she did not impart to Ahab; she kept it to her-self, regarding it as a secret for reasons that will become appar-ent later. In the Bible this particular character [upon whose innermost being Elijah's spirit worked] is known by the name of Naboth. We thus see that according to the investigations of spiritual science we must recognize in the Naboth of the Bible the physical bearer of the spiritual individuality of Elijah.

It was in those days that a great famine came upon the land, and there were many who hungered. Naboth, in certain ways, also experienced want and distress. At times such as these, when not only does hunger prevail, as was assuredly the case in Palestine, but when on every side there is also a feeling of infi-nite pity for those who suffer, the conditions are especially favorable for the entry of latent soul forces into one already prepared through destiny or *karma*. It is alone through these hidden powers of the soul that human beings may raise them-selves to the level of such a mission as we have outlined.

Let us clearly picture what takes place deep within the being under such circumstances and thus gain an understanding of the manner in which Naboth's soul was affected. In the initial stage there is an inner progressive change or unfoldment marked by an important period of self-education and self-development. It is extremely difficult to describe those inner experiences of the soul that tend to raise it to greater spiritual heights while the personality is becoming imbued with the forces by means of which it will be enabled to look upon the world of spirit. The power of divine spiritual vision must next be called into being, so that there may arise the wis-dom necessary to the inception of all vital impulses destined to be implanted in the stream of human evolution. A verbal description is here the more difficult because never once have those who have undergone an experience of this nature, especially in olden times, come to such a state of apperception that they could outline their impressions in a precise and lucid manner. What actually happens may be stated to be somewhat as follows: The clairvoyant development of the soul is accomplished through different stages. In the case of a being such as Naboth, it would naturally occur that his first inner experience would be the clear apprehension of the following definite concept: "The spiritual power that is ordained to descend upon humanity will now shine forth in me, and I am its appointed receptacle." Next would come this thought: "I must henceforth do all that in me lies so that the force within my being may find true and proper expression and that I may acquire those qualities that shall fit me to cope with every form of trial and experience that may come upon me. Thus shall I know how to impart the power of divine impulse to my fellows in proper fashion."

It is in this way that the spiritual and clairvoyant development of a personality such as I have described must go forward—step by step. When a suitable predetermined stage has been reached, then follow certain definite and noticeable signs that manifest within the soul. These are also of the nature of inner experiences; they are neither dreams nor visions, for they owe their origin to and are dependent upon the soul's actual growth and unfoldment. Pictorial images appear; they indicate that inner progress has now so far advanced that the particular personality in question may reasonably believe that his soul has indeed acquired new powers. Taken alone, these images do not necessarily have much connection with the reality of those experiences through which the soul is passing. They are merely symbols, such as may come during the sleep state. But in a certain way they are typical symbols, similar to those that occur under certain conditions when we have very distinct and positive dreams. For instance, a person suffering from palpitation of the heart may, during sleep, be under an illusion that heat is emanating from some glowing source, as, for instance, a hot stove. In like manner when the soul has gained this or that special clairvoyant power, then will come corresponding definite experiences in the form of visionary manifestations.

In the case of Naboth, the first event of this nature brought with it a full realization of all that is implied in the following:

> Thou art the chosen one, through whom it shall be proclaimed that human beings may still believe in the ancient Yahweh God and that they must hold fast to this faith, even though it outwardly seemeth that because of the sore tribulation come upon the land, the current of life's happenings be set against such trust. Humanity must now rest in peace till times may mend. For though it is the will of Yahweh, the God of old, to come with affliction, nevertheless shall humanity again rejoice—but they must be steadfast of faith in the Lord God."

It was evident to Naboth that this proclamation that should come through him was undoubtedly the expression of a true and unswerving force, carrying a conviction that lay deep within his soul. This experience stood out vividly as something more than a mere vision. Then before his soul there arose an image of God himself, in that form and manner in which it was within his power to picture him. The presence said, "Go thou to King Ahab, and say unto him that in the god Yahweh must ye have faith until such time as he may again bring rain upon the earth"—in other words, until conditions should improve. Naboth realized the nature of his mission; he knew also that from that time on he must devote himself to the further unfolding of that power of soul through which he might apprehend and interpret all that was yet to be presented to his spiritual vision. He resolved that he would shun no sacrifice, but as much as he could he would share in the sufferings of those who were exposed to the greatest measure of want and starvation during that time. Thus it came about that Naboth also hungered, but he did not seek thereby to rise to a higher spiritual state. Such a process, I would state, is most certainly not to be recommended as a step toward higher spiritual knowledge and understanding. He hungered because of an impulse that made him desire to suffer as others did. He thus want to share in the common fate, and it was his earnest wish to take upon himself a measure of adversity greater than that endured by those around him.

The soul of Naboth was given over to unceasing inner contemplation of that God who had revealed Himself to him in the manner described, and his thoughts were ever concentrated upon this Diety. The spiritual science of our time would say that throughout his meditations he devoted himself entirely and of his own free will to holding this divine concept in the very center of his soul. That he acted rightly in doing so was made clear to him by a sign that came during an inner vision. This vision was again more positive than any of merely dreamlike character, for an image of that God who dwelled within his soul appeared before him, and it was full of life. A voice said, "Abide in patience and endure all things, for he who feedeth humanity and thee also will surely provide that which thou needest. But thou must ever hold to a true faith in the soul's eternal life." In this vision, which was of greater pictorial reality than any that came before, it appeared to him [whom we may now, under the singular conditions that prevailed, term *Elijah-Naboth*] that he was led by a hermit to the brook called Cherith, where he concealed himself and drank of the waters of the brook so long as any remained, and that he was nourished, so far as the conditions prevailing at the time permitted, by food the Lord provided. It further seemed to him during the vision that through the special mercy of God, this nutriment was brought by ravens. Thus did [Elijah-Naboth] receive confirmation of the truth of the most important among those inner experiences he was destined to encounter. It was next ordained that [Naboth] should pass through a more advanced stage of development in relation to the activities of the hidden soul forces—and we know that he endeavored to immerse himself yet more deeply (as we would now explain it) in that condition of intensive contemplation that lay at the foundation of his spiritual progress, the character of which we have already described.

This state of profound meditation fraught with inner-life experiences assumed the following form: Naboth pondered thus: "If you would indeed become worthy of that mission that will shine in upon humanity because of this wholly new concept of God's image, then must you change utterly the nature of your inner being, even to the most profound of its forces, so that you are no more as you have been. You will subdue the soul that dwells in you and, through those deeper powers within, bring to your inner Ego a new life, for it may no longer remain as it now is. [You must uplift its quality.]" Under the influence of thoughts such as these [Naboth] worked intensively upon his soul, striving within that he might bring about this essential transformation of his Ego and thus become worthy to stand in the presence of that God who had revealed himself before him.

Then came to [Elijah-Naboth] yet another experience that was, however, only in part a vision. Because it was not entirely of the nature of an inner soul happening, there being other content, it must be regarded as of less spiritual significance. It is always the pure inner workings of the soul that are of truest and greatest import. In this vision, it appeared to him that his God, who had again manifested, set him upon a journey to Zarephath (1 Kings 17:9), and in that place he met a widow who had a son. He saw represented, or personified as it were, in the fate of this widow and her son the manner and way in which he was now to live. It seemed to his spiritual sight that their food was almost spent; the food they had was about to be consumed, after which they would die. Then it was that he spoke to the widow as in a dream, a vision, using in effect those same words that day by day and week by week, throughout his solitary meditations, he had repeated over and over again to his own soul: "Fear not. From the meal that remains prepare the repast that must be made ready for you and your son and for me also. In all that may yet come to pass trust alone in that God who creates both joy and sorrow and in whom we must ever abide in faith."

In this dreamlike vision it was clearly impressed upon [Elijah-Naboth] that the barrel of meal would not become empty nor would the cruse of oil fail, for the oil and the meal would be renewed. It is worth noting that at this point his whole soul state, which had become, so to speak, fully developed and perfected with regard to his individual character, expressed itself in the vision in such manner, that it seemed to him as if his personality went to live in the upper part of the house that belonged to the widow. The inner truth was that his own soul had, one might say, risen to a higher level and achieved a more advanced stage of development.

It next appeared to [Elijah-Naboth], again as in a vision, that the son of the widow lay dead. This we must regard as merely a symbolic representation of the fact that [Naboth] had overcome and slain the Ego that had been his up to that time. Then the subconscious forces in his soul cried out: "What will you do now?" For a while [Elijah-Naboth] stood helpless and perplexed, but he was able to regain his self-control through the medium of the power that had always lived and flowed within his innermost being and to plunge yet more profoundly into the consideration of those conditions that called for such deep and earnest contemplation. It then happened that after the widow's son was dead, she reproached him. This signifies that his subconscious spirit reproached him, in other words, aroused in him a misgiving of this nature: "My old Ego-consciousness has now left me—what am I to do?" In the description given of these events, it is stated that he took the child to himself and plunged unhesitatingly still further into the depths of his soul. We are told that power was given to him through which he brought the dead son once more to life. Then did he gain more courage to stimulate and enliven the new Ego that was now his by virtue of those qualities that were in the Ego that he had lost.

From that time on [Elijah-Naboth] continued to develop and mature the hidden forces of his soul so that it might acquire that inner strength necessary to come before the outer world and utter those words all must hear. But, in the first place and above everything, he had to stand before King Ahab and bring to a crisis the matter that had now to be decided, namely, the victory of the new Yahweh concept over those beliefs that the king himself accepted and which, owing to the weakness of the times, had become generally acknowledged among the people.

It came about that while Ahab was making a round of his empire, anxiously observing the signs of want and distress, the personality [whom we have called Elijah-Naboth] approached him. No man knew from whence he came; certainly the king had no idea. And there was a strangeness in the manner of his speech that affected the soul of Ahab, who was not, however, aware that this man was his neighbor. More strongly than ever did the king experience that feeling of awe and dread that had always come upon him when reference was made to that great spirit known in the Bible as Elijah the prophet. Then it was that the king spoke and said: "Art you he that troubles Israel?" And Elijah-Naboth replied, "No, not I, but you yourself it is who brings misfortune and evil upon the people, and it must now be determined to which god they shall turn."

So it was that a great multitude of the tribe of Israel assembled on Mount Carmel so that final judgment should be made between the god of Ahab and the God of Elijah. The decision was to be brought about by means of an external sign, but such a sign as all might plainly discern and clearly understand. To enter into details concerning these matters at the present time would, however, take us too far. It was arranged that the priests and prophets of Baal, the name by which the god of King Ahab was known, should be the first to offer a sacrifice. The people would then wait and see if the performance of certain sacrificial rites (religious exercises in which the priests, through the medium of music and dancing, worked themselves up into a state of singular ecstasy) would lead to any communication or influence being imparted to the multitude. In other words, the people were to judge whether or not, by virtue of inherent divine powers possessed by the priests, any sign was given of the might and potency of their god.

The sacrificial beast was brought to the altar. It was to be decided if in truth the priests of Baal were endowed with an inner force, such as would stir the multitude. Then Elijah-Naboth raised up his voice and said, "This thing must now be determined—I stand alone, while opposed to me are the four hundred and fifty prophets of Baal. We shall see how strong is their hold upon the people and how great is that power which is in me." The sacrifice was performed and everything possible done in order to transmit to the multitude a potent influence from the priests, that all should believe in the god Baal. The ecstatic exercises were carried to such lengths that the hands and other parts of the body were cut with knives until the blood flowed, so as to increase still further the awesome character of the spectacle evoked by these followers of Baal under the frenzied stimulus of the dancing and the music. But behold! There was no sign, for Elijah-Naboth was there, and the spirit within him was at work. In words insufficient of expression, one might say that while Elijah-Naboth stood near at hand, he caused a great spiritual power to flow forth from his being so that he overcame and swept away all things opposed to him. In this case, you must not, however, imagine to yourselves the exercise of any kind of magic.

Elijah-Naboth then prepared his sacrifice. He made an offering to his God using the full force of his soul, that soul which had passed through all those trials we have already described. The sacrifice was consummated and achieved the fullness of its purpose, for the souls and the hearts of the people were stirred. The priests of Baal, the four hundred and fifty opponents of Elijah, were driven to admit defeat. *They were destroyed in their very souls by that which they had desired*—killed, as it were, by Elijah-Naboth. Elijah-Naboth had won the day!

These events were in some ways similar to those that I have endeavored to portray in my book entitled *Mysticism after Modernism*.[13] While speaking of [the German mystic theologian] Johannes Tauler, it is there related that for a considerable period during his life he was known as a remarkable and trenchant preacher and that at one time he gave himself up to a particular form of training, after which, upon his return to the pulpit, he exercised upon one occasion such an extraordinary influence upon his congregation that we are told some forty persons collapsed as if dead. This signifies that their innermost beings were touched and that they were overcome by the sympathetic action of a special power emanating from that great divine. With such an example before us, we need no longer imagine that the Bible account concerning Ahab and Elijah is a mere exaggeration, for it is at all events entirely confirmed by the researches of spiritual science.

What follows as the natural outcome of all these events? I have already described the character and peculiar nature of Jezebel. She was quite aware of the fact that the man who had done all these things was their neighbor and that he was to be found living close at hand, that is, when he was not mysteriously

---

13. *Mystics after Modernism: Discovering the Seeds of a New Science in the Renaissance* presents the leading thoughts of Meister Eckhart, Johannes Tauler, Heinrich Suso, Jan van Ruysbroeck, Nicholas of Cusa, Agrippa of Nettesheim, Paracelsus, Valentin Weigel, Jacob Boehme, Giordano Bruno, and Angelus Silesius (Anthroposophic Press, Great Barrington, MA, 2000).

absent. What did Elijah-Naboth know and realize from that moment? He knew that Jezebel was powerful and that she had discovered his secret. In other words, he felt that henceforth his outer physical life was no longer safe. He must therefore prepare for death in the near future, for Jezebel would certainly bring about his destruction.

King Ahab went home and, as related in the Bible, told Jezebel about the events that had taken place on Mount Carmel. [spiritual science tells us, that] Jezebel said, "I will do to Elijah that which he did to your four hundred and fifty prophets." Who could understand these words spoken by Jezebel [and reflected in I Kings 19:2] were it not for the investigations made by spiritual science, in whose light their meaning seems almost self-evident. [As a result of these researches, it is quite clear—and this point has always been obscure—why it was that Jezebel brought about the death of Naboth when in reality she sought to destroy Elijah. From spiritual science, however, we realize that she sent her threatening message to Elijah-Naboth, because by virtue of her clairvoyant powers she knew full well that the physical body of Naboth was the bearer of Elijah's spirit.]

It now became necessary for Elijah to form definite plans whereby he could avoid being immediately done to death as a result of Jezebel's revenge. He at once had to arrange that in case of this event happening, his spirit could still continue to carry on his teachings and exert its influence upon humanity. When next he communed inwardly with his soul and while in a state of intense inner contemplation, he questioned himself thus: "What shall I do that I may find a successor to fulfill my mission in this physical world should my death indeed be brought about through the vengeance of Jezebel?" Then, a new revelation came to him, in which his inner vision was directed toward a certain quite definite personality to whom Elijah-Naboth might pass on all that he had to bestow upon mankind—this personality was Elisha.[14] You may think it possible that Elijah had previously known Elisha; whether such was the case or not is a matter of little importance. What is of moment is the fact that it was the spirit that pointed to the way and that he heard through an inner illumination these words: "Initiate this man into your secrets."

We are further told, with the clarity that marks the statements of spiritual science concerning ancient religious records, that Elijah-Naboth had a very special mission to fulfill and that the divine element that was about to descend upon Elisha would be of the same spirit as had previously been predominant in Elijah. It was in Damascus that Elisha was to be sought, and in that place he would receive this great spiritual illumination, which would come to him in the same way as that glorious divine light that flowed in upon Saint Paul at a later period. Soon after Elijah had chosen his successor, the vengeance of Jezebel fell upon him. For Jezebel turned the thoughts of her lord toward Naboth, their neighbor, and spoke to Ahab somewhat in this fashion: "Listen to me; this neighbor is a pious man whose mind is filled with ideas concerning Elijah. It would perhaps be well to remove him from this vicinity, for he is one of the most important of his followers, and upon him much depends."

The king knew nothing whatever about the secret that surrounded Naboth, but he was quite aware by this time that he was indeed a faithful adherent of Elijah's and gave heed to his

---

14. See the addendum to this lecture, p. 175ff.

words. Jezebel next urged Ahab to try to induce Naboth to come over to his side, either by methods of persuasion or, if necessary, by exercising his power of kingly authority. She said: "It would be a great blow to the schemes and projects of this man Elijah if by any means it were possible to draw him away from his intents." Jezebel knew quite well, however, that all her talk was the merest fiction; what she really desired was to induce her lord to take some kind of definite and effective action. It was not this particular move in which she was interested; her mind was bent upon a plot that was to follow. Thus the advice she tendered was of the nature of a subterfuge. After Jezebel had spoken in this way to Ahab, the king went to Naboth and spoke with him. Naboth, however, would not regard what he said and replied, "Never shall those things come to pass that you desire."

In the Bible the position is so represented that this neighbor of Ahab's is described as possessing a vineyard that the king coveted and sought to acquire. According to this account (I Kings 21:3), Naboth said to Ahab: "The Lord forbid it me, that I should give the inheritance of my fathers unto thee." In reality, however, the actual inheritance to which reference is made was of quite another kind than that which Naboth declined to surrender. Nevertheless, Jezebel used this incident as the foundation of her revenge. She deliberately gave false counsel so that the king might be disconcerted and then angered by Naboth's refusal. That such was the case becomes evident when we read that passage in the Bible (I Kings 21:4) where it is written: "And Ahab came into his house heavy and displeased because of the word which Naboth the Jezreelite had spoken to him: for he had said, I will not give thee the inheritance of my fathers. And he laid him down upon his bed, and turned away his face, and would eat no bread." Think of that! Merely because the king could not obtain a certain vineyard in his neighborhood, he refused to eat! We can begin to understand such statements only when we are in a position to investigate the facts underlying them.

It was at this point that Jezebel took definite steps to bring about her revenge. She started by arranging that a feast be given to which Naboth should be invited and at which he was to be an especially honored guest (I Kings 21:12). Naboth could not refuse to be present, and at this feast it was planned that he be afforded an opportunity of expressing himself freely. Jezebel was truly gifted with clairvoyant insight. With the others Naboth could easily cope; with them he could measure forces. But Jezebel had the power to bring ruin upon him. She introduced false witnesses, who declared that "Naboth did deny [blaspheme] God and the king." It was in this manner that she contrived to bring about his murder, as is related in the Bible (I Kings, 21:13). Henceforth the outer physical personality of Elijah was dead and was no more seen upon the face of the external world.

Because of all that had happened, the deep forces in Ahab's soul were stirred. He was confronted with the grave question of his destiny, while at the same time he experienced a strange and unusual foreboding. Then Elijah, whom he had always regarded with feelings of awe, appeared as in a vision and revealed to him plainly how the matter stood. Here we have an actual spiritual experience, in which Ahab was accused by the spirit form of Elijah (subsequent to his death) of having virtually himself murdered Naboth—this Naboth-Elijah. The connection with the latter personality he could but dimly realize; nevertheless, Ahab was definitely termed his murderer. In the

Bible we can read the dreadful words that fell upon his soul during that awe-inspiring prophecy, when the spirit form said, "In the place where dogs licked the blood of Naboth shall dogs lick thy blood, even thine' (I Kings 21:19). Then came yet another dire prophetic utterance: "The dogs shall eat Jezebel by the wall of Jezreel" (I Kings 21:23).

We now know that these predictions belonged to a class that finds ultimate fulfilment. For subsequently, when King Ahab went forth to battle against the Syrians, he was wounded; his blood ran out of the wound into the chariot, and he died. When the chariot was being washed, dogs came and licked up his blood (I Kings 22:35, 38). Later on, after a further course of events had made Jehu ruler of Jezreel, Jezebel was seen as she stood at a window; she was seized and thrown down, and dogs tore her to pieces and actually devoured her before the walls of the city (2 Kings 9:30–37). I have touched lightly upon these matters because our time is short and they are of no special importance to us just now. You will find that the subject I am about to consider is of much greater moment.

He whom Elijah-Naboth had elected to be his successor had then to develop and perfect his inner being, even as Elijah-Naboth himself had done. But this spiritual unfolding was brought about in a different way. For the pupil it was in some ways less difficult than it had been for his teacher, since all the power that Elijah-Naboth had acquired through constant upward striving was now at his disciple's disposal, and he had the help and support of his great master. Elijah-Naboth influenced Elisha in the same way as the individualities of those who have passed through the portals of death may at times act upon humanity, namely, by means of a special form of spiritual activity emanating directly from the spirit world. The divine force that descended upon Elisha was similar in nature to the glorious inspiration that Christ Jesus himself gave to his disciples after his resurrection. Elisha's subsequent experiences were directly related to this divine power that continued to flow forth from Elijah even after his death and to affect all who might give themselves up to its potent influence. With Elisha, his experience was such that the living form of his great master appeared before his soul and said, "I will go forth with thee out of Gilgal."

At this point I quote the Bible literally, where it says (2 Kings 2:1), "And it came to pass, when the Lord would take up Elijah into heaven by a whirlwind, that Elijah went with Elisha from Gilgal." Gilgal is not a place or locality, and it is not intended in the Bible that it should be taken as such. The word *Gilgal* merely signifies the act of moving in a circuitous path while revolving, as in waltzing. This technical expression refers to the roundabout course of the soul's life during those periods in which it is incarnated in the flesh and passes from one physical body to another; that is the true significance of "Gilgal."

It need cause you no surprise that the results obtained through spiritual science show that Elisha, by virtue of soul experiences gained through inner contemplation and absolute devotion, could be in the actual presence of Elijah in a higher state or world. This was made possible not because of the forces latent in his physical nature but through those more exalted powers he possessed. While Elisha was thus uplifted, the steps that he had to take toward his soul's development were pointed out to him by the spirit of Elijah, who constantly drew his attention to the difficulties he would encounter on the path he must follow. The way led upward and onward, step by step, to a stage where he would first feel himself unified with that divine spirit always flowing forth from his great teacher Elijah.

The names, apparently referring to places that have been chosen [in the Bible, such as Beth-el and Jericho (2 Kings 2:2, 4)], are not to be taken as designating localities but in their literal sense, signifying conditions of the soul. For instance, Elijah says, "I will now take me to Beth-el." This statement was made to Elisha in a vision, but to him it was more than a mere vision. Then, again, as if counselling him, the spirit of Elijah spoke and said, "It were better to remain here." The true significance of this statement is this: "Consider whether you possess the strength to go with me further" [referring to the spiritual path]. The vision then continues with an incident in which we again find something in the nature of an exhortation and warning. All the sons of the prophets who were his colleagues in the spirit stood about Elisha and cautioned him, and those who were initiated into the mystery and knew that at times he could indeed ascend to the higher regions, where the spirit of Elijah conversed with him, admonished him and told him that this time he would not be able to follow Elijah— "Knowest thou that the Lord will take away thy master from thy head to-day?" (2 Kings 2:3). His answer was "Hold ye your peace." But to the spirit of Elijah he said, "As the Lord liveth, and as thy soul liveth, I will not leave thee." Elijah spoke again and said, "The Lord hath sent me to Jericho" [2 Kings 2:4).

Once again this dialogue is repeated [and the word *Jordan* is introduced (2 Kings 2:6)], after which Elijah asks, "Ask what I shall do for thee." The reply Elisha gave is recorded in the

Bible but in such a manner that we have to drag out its proper meaning, for it is rendered incorrectly. The words are these: "I pray thee let a double portion of thy spirit be upon me" (2 Kings 2:9); the actual answer, however, was this: "I desire that thy spirit shall enter and dwell as a second spirit within my soul." The essence of Elisha's request, as understood by Elijah, was somewhat as follows: Elisha had asked that his soul be stirred to its very depths and enlivened so that he might awaken to a full consciousness of its true relation to the spirit of his master. It could then of its own powers bring about enlightenment concerning spiritual revelation, even as had been the case during the physical life of his great teacher.

Elijah spoke again and said to this effect: I must now ascend into the higher realms; if thou art able to perceive my spirit as it rises upward, then hast thou attained thy desire and my power will enter in unto thee. And Elisha indeed saw the spirit of Elijah as he "went up by a whirlwind into heaven" (2 Kings 2:11), and the mantle of Elijah fell down [upon him], which was a symbol denoting the spiritual force in which he must now enwrap himself. Here, then, we have a spiritual vision that indicated and at the same time caused Elisha to realize that he might now indeed become the true successor of Elijah. In the Bible (2 Kings 2:15) we read, "And when the sons of the prophets which were to view at Jericho saw him, they said, The Spirit of Elijah doth rest on Elisha. And they came to meet him, and bowed themselves to the ground before him." This passage points to the fact that the Word of the Lord had become so mighty in Elisha that it was filled with the same force that the sons of the prophets had experienced with Elijah, and they realized that the spirit of Elijah-Naboth truly lived on in the being of Elisha.

In previous lectures I described the methods employed by
spiritual science; as we proceed, they will be further elucidated.
The foregoing account gives expression to its testimony regarding the actual events that took place in Elijah's time and also
concerning the impulse to humanity that flowed forth from
that great prophet and his successor, Elisha. This impulse
always tended toward the renewing and uplifting of the ancient
Yahweh faith. It is characteristic of that ancient period that incidents such as we have portrayed and which could be understood
only by the initiated were represented to the mass of the people
(who were quite incapable of comprehending them in their true
form) in such a manner as to render them intelligible and, at the
same time, to cause them to work upon and to influence the
soul. The method to which I refer is that of parables or miracle
stories. But what seems to us so truly amazing, in the highest
spiritual sense, is that out of such allegorical narratives there
should have been evolved an account like that relating to Elijah,
Elisha, and Naboth, as told in the Bible.

In those days it was the custom to use the parable form
when speaking to all who could not understand or realize the
supreme glory of the impulse that had come from the souls of
these great ones, spiritual beings who of themselves had first
to undergo many inner experiences deeply hidden from
human external vision and apprehension. Thus it was that the
people were told, as may be gathered from the Bible, that Elijah lived in the time of King Ahab and that during a period of
famine the god Jahveh appeared before him and [as spiritual
science tells us] commanded him to go to the King Ahab and
say to him: "As the Lord God of Israel liveth, before whom I
stand, there shall not be dew nor rain these years, but according to my word" (I Kings 17:1). The account in the Bible

continues as follows: "And the word of the Lord came unto him saying, Get thee hence, and turn thee eastward, and hide thyself by the brook Cherith, that is before Jordan. And it shall be, that thou shalt drink of the brook; and I have commanded the ravens to feed thee there" (I Kings 17:2–4). These things came about; when the brook was dried up, God sent Elijah to Zarephath (I Kings 17:9). "In the third year" he was commanded to set out and appear before King Ahab (I Kings 18:1) and to cause the four hundred and fifty prophets of Baal to be called to a final decision (I Kings 18:19). I have previously referred to all this when presenting the facts as obtained through spiritual science.

Next comes a wonderful picture of the events that actually took place on Mount Carmel (I Kings 18:20–39), which I have described. Then follows the story of how Naboth (who was in reality the bearer of the spirit of Elijah) was to be robbed of his vineyard by Ahab and of how Jezebel brought ruin upon him (I Kings 21:1–14). From the Bible account alone, we cannot understand how Jezebel could possibly have accomplished the destruction of Elijah in accordance with her threatening utterance to King Ahab (see page 162), namely, that she would do to Elijah that which he did to Ahab's four hundred and fifty prophets. The story tells us that she merely effected the death of Naboth. As a matter of fact, however, she actually brought destruction to the being in whom dwelt at that time the spirit of Elijah. This point would undoubtedly escape the notice of any ordinary biblical student, for in the Bible it merely states that Elijah ascended into heaven (2 Kings 2:11).

If, as is intimated in the Bible, Jezebel's desire was to do to Elijah what he had done to the four hundred and fifty prophets of Baal, she certainly accomplished her end and brought about his ruin in a most remarkable manner![15] I would here state that there are some graphic portrayals relative to the dim past that can be rightly understood only when illumined by the bright radiance that flows from the deep sources of spiritual research.

It is not possible in a single lecture to bring forward further evidence and proofs concerning these matters. If, however, those among my audience who may still feel that they cannot look upon the pronouncements of spiritual science as other than hypotheses would but criticize without prejudice and set about comparing the various statements made with facts obtained through the medium of external science, I should feel entirely satisfied. Although it is true that if spiritual methods of research are not employed, we cannot hope to reach final and positive conclusions, it will still be found that the truth of spiritual science is confirmed by the results of orthodox scientific investigations and the proper exercise of individual intelligence.

When we study the personality and period of the prophet Elijah, it becomes clear that the impulses and primal causes that

---

15. It has been previously stated (page 161) that through Elijah-Naboth the prophets of Baal were "destroyed in their very souls by that which they had desired." Elijah longed that his spirit might continue to be active in the being of Naboth, and it was this very wish that caused Jezebel to set about his ruin and thus, as it were, to destroy Elijah in his very soul. It was not merely physical death to which Jezebel referred when she sent her message to Elijah, saying, "So let the gods do to me, and more also, if I make not thy life as the life of one of them by tomorrow about this time" (1 Kings 19:2). She referred to a kind of spiritual death, which would break forever that mysterious and sacred union between Elijah and Naboth that it was her aim to sever. She knew quite well, by virtue of her clairvoyant powers, that she could hope to accomplish this end and "destroy Elijah in his very soul" only by bringing about the material dissolution of Naboth, the bearer of Elijah's spirit. Thus we find that if we read Jezebel's message anew, in the light thrown of spiritual science, its purport becomes at once intelligible.

underlie and bring about human events are in no way limited to those occurrences that are outwardly apparent and therefore find a place in the records of external history. By far the most important and significant happenings connected with human existence have their actual origin and are matured with respect to a primary stage within the confines of the soul. The outcome of this fundamental process next finds expression in the outer world, spreading its influence further and further among the people. Although these days it is inconceivable that a mysterious personality such as we have portrayed, and known only through rumor, could dwell in our midst in the guise of a simple and homely neighbor without all the facts becoming known, in olden times such a circumstance was undoubtedly possible. We have learned that throughout all human evolution it is precisely those forces that are of greatest power and intensity which operate in an obscure and secret fashion.

From what has been said, it is clear that through the influence of the prophet Elijah, human beings were raised to a higher spiritual level and became more and more imbued with Jahveh thoughts and concepts. We also realize that the life and deeds of that great patriarch, when viewed in the proper manner, must be regarded as forming an epoch of supreme import to humanity. Further investigation and research will assuredly prove that [by means of the methods of spiritual science] a new light has been thrown upon the momentous happenings of a bygone age and on the events that ultimately led to the founding of Christianity. We know that through realities of this nature, born of the spirit world, we can draw nearer to an understanding of those fundamental forces and impulses that have been active in the course of the evolution of humanity and therefore appear to us of such great significance and moment.

Then, with enhanced knowledge, we shall realize that even as these basic actors have operated in remote antiquity, so must they continue to work on in our present period. Never can we read the deep secrets of the life around us if we have no clear concept of the inner nature and purport of those singular events that have taken place in the dim and distant past.

External history, which is garnered solely from the outer world, does not enlighten us concerning matters of greatest and most vital import. It is here that the words of Goethe so fittingly apply—words that if they are read with a touch of deeper meaning become a call to humanity, urging us to profound inner spiritual contemplation. For it is thus that human beings may enter upon that quest which alone can spring from the soul's most hidden depths and learn to apprehend the divine spirit that exists and abides in all nature. The wonderful example of the prophet Elijah and his period, as it shines forth in our spiritual firmament, stands as evidence of the truth of Goethe's words, which in slightly modified form, are as follows:

History will not permit that veil to be withdrawn,
Which hides her secrets from the light of our new day.
That which she chooses from thy spirit to conceal,
Canst thou ne'er wrest from parchment script, nor canst thou say,
What message lies secreted 'neath those mystic signs,
Inscribed on bronze, or fashioned deep in stone or clay.[16]

---

16. Geheimnisvoll am lichten Tag der Gegenwart,
    Lässt Geschichte sich des Schleiers nicht berauben.
    Was sie deinem Geist nicht offenbaren mag,
    Das zwingst du ihr nicht aus Pergamenten
    Und nicht aus Zeichen, die eingeschrieben sind
    In Erz und Ton und Stein.

* * *

ADDENDUM

In this lecture, which was delivered in Berlin in 1911, it will be noticed that in some cases the name Elijah-Naboth is found in places where only Elijah is mentioned in the Bible. The reason for this apparent inconsistency becomes at once evident when we take a general view of the circumstances and singular relationship that existed between Elijah and Naboth and what we might term a duality of being as expressed in Elijah-Naboth. Let us therefore briefly consider the events portrayed in the order in which they took place.

At the time of Ahab, the Hebrew people were for the most part so far sunk in materialism that there was danger not only that disaster would overtake them but also that the actual course of the spiritual evolution of humankind might be hindered; the matter had gone to such a length as to call for divine intervention. For this reason it was ordained that Elijah, whom we must regard as a truly exalted spirit, should descend upon the earth and that his mission would be to turn the hearts of the people once more to Yahweh and to determine his (Elijah's) successor. This mission we may look upon as being accomplished in four stages.

At first the spirit of Elijah worked in mysterious ways, for he appeared among the people now here and now there; no man knew from whence he came. In those days the masses were often moved in matters concerning religious thought by engendering feelings of awe and wonder, and by so doing Elijah established a definite and powerful influence among the minds of the community. He thus prepared the people to witness the sign of the spirit that it was decreed should be imparted. Only through a great manifestation of divine force could the nation, in that material state into which it had fallen, be brought back to Yahweh, the ancient God of the Hebrews.

In the second stage of Elijah's mission we come upon the simple landowner Naboth. In order to create the utmost possible impression at the time when the supreme revelation of spiritual power should take place, it was essential that a multitude be present. But for this thing to happen, it was necessary to gain the consent of the king. Now Naboth lived near Ahab and might on occasion obtain audience with him; in this manner he could aid Elijah in the maturing of his plans. Elijah therefore so worked upon the innermost soul of Naboth that he became "the bearer of his spirit" and did according to his word. Thus did Elijah's spirit find expression through the outer form of Naboth and bring influence to bear upon the king that all should be made ready for the people to be gathered together when the moment was at hand for the sign to be given. It is the dual state of Naboth's being while the spirit of Elijah was dominant and worked within him that has been termed *Elijah-Naboth*.

Ahab was not truly clairvoyant and had no suspicion of all that had occurred. On that occasion when he met Elijah-Naboth and said to him, "Art thou he that troubleth Israel?" (I Kings 18:17), he thought it was only Naboth who was speaking and that it was he who would turn the people against the gods of Baal. Ahab at that time merely knew of Elijah through indefinite rumor. But it was the voice of Elijah the prophet speaking *through* Naboth that answered the king—it was Elijah-Naboth that spoke. It is because the ancient writer who portrayed this incident did not realize the singular spiritual and clairvoyant conditions, and therefore did not fully understand the circumstances, that the name of Elijah alone appears in this account, as in other Bible accounts connected with the events that took place in those days.

We find a similar difference in the names occurring in the description of the happening on Mount Carmel, when the people were assembled to judge between Jehovah and the gods of Baal. It was then that the third stage of Elijah's mission was fulfilled. In the lecture it is stated that it was Elijah-Naboth who was present on

Mount Carmel and that it was he who "won the day," but the Bible narrative tells us that it was Elijah himself who overcame the prophets of Baal. The reason for this apparent inconsistency can be seen from the following considerations.

It was Elijah-Naboth who, when all had come, stood forth and said, "This thing must now be determined—I stand alone while opposed to me are the four hundred and fifty prophets of Baal." But Elijah, who was granted special spiritual powers at that moment, so ordered the matter that while the king saw before him merely the outer form of the man Naboth, the people were impressed with the spiritual being and personality of Elijah. In the Bible the narrator realized the circumstances *as the multitude had apprehended them* and therefore spoke only of Elijah, being unaware at that time that Naboth was "the bearer of his spirit."

Jezebel was not present at Mount Carmel, because she was conscious that she could not cope directly with Elijah. Through her clairvoyant powers she was cognizant of all that had come to pass, and she knew full well that the spirit of the great prophet would be all powerful in that place. In other words, she clearly understood that if she went to Mount Carmel, she would there have to do with Elijah-Naboth and not merely with the simple landowner. She thought, however, that if she could only effect the physical death of Naboth, she might put an end to Elijah's influence.

Next came the fourth stage of Elijah's mission. He must seek a successor and do so before Jezebel brought about the death of Naboth, for when the outer form of Naboth should be destroyed, Elijah must return to the divine spirit realms. At that point in the lecture (page 163) where it states that Elijah communed with his soul and asked the question "What shall I do that I may find a successor to fulfill my mission in this physical world should my death indeed be brought about through the vengeance of Jezebel?" he is referring to the material death of Naboth and to the possible premature ending of the impulse he had wrought. Further, we are told that spiritual science states that "Elijah-Naboth had a very special mission to fulfill and that the divine element that was about to descend upon Elisha would be of the same spirit as had previously been predominant in Elijah." We are told that "it was in Damascus that Elisha was to be sought." In the Bible (I Kings 19:15, 16) we find these words: "And the Lord said unto him [Elijah], Go, return on thy way to the wilderness of Damascus. . . . and Elisha the son of Shaphat of Abel-meholah shalt thou anoint to be prophet in thy room." The actual command to seek out Elisha was given in a vision to Elijah, as is indicated both in the lecture and in I Kings 19:12, 13. Spiritual science, however, tells us that it was *Elijah-Naboth* who made the journey. This is quite comprehensible when we realize that in Elijah-Naboth, Elisha—by virtue of his advanced spirituality—would know and commune with the spirit being of Elijah. Here again it is for reasons similar to those already advanced that in the Bible the name of Elijah only occurs, while in the lecture Elijah-Naboth is mentioned.

In all such cases it will be found, if we but look deeply into the matter, that the statements of spiritual science are in truth not in any way at variance with those things written in the Bible.

6. CHRIST

and the Twentieth Century

It cannot be denied, even by those who have made only a slight study of spiritual life, that the subject chosen for our consideration today has aroused an interest in the widest circles. We might add that this desire for knowledge is of a scientific character. On the other hand, there seems to be an ever-increasing tendency toward the formation of a world philosophy in which such questions as are associated with the name of Christ find no true and proper place. A previous lecture I gave some few weeks ago here under the title "The Origin of the Human Being" and a continuation of the same on "The Origin of the Animal World" will doubtless have made clear to you a point to which I shall now again draw your attention. In every age, including the present period, the general conceptions and sentiments concerning such fundamental questions as the origin of the human being and others of a similar nature, including those relative to that being to whom the name of Christ has been given, are directly rooted in and dependent upon the accepted concepts of some previous age.

We have already seen while considering various matters connected with the origin of humanity that as a matter of fact those theoretical ideas and conceptions that have sprung from the

general mode of thought prevailing in our time are fundamentally at variance with the actual results of scientific research. On
the other hand, it is just in this relation that we find that the
conclusions arrived at through the medium of spiritual science,
which traces the human being's origin back to spiritual forms
and not merely to that which is external and physically percepti-
ble, are in full harmony with the results obtained in the field of
natural science. Perhaps nowhere do we find this want of accord
so marked between the current cosmic concept prevalent in the
thoughts and hearts of the people of our day and that which science has been constrained to adopt as in the case of the Christ
conception. This divergence may well be due to the fact that
these questions belong to the greatest of all those concerning
the cosmos. However, since the coming of the Christ movement
into the world's history, human beings' power of conception
concerning the Christ-being and the form it has taken have ever
been such as was best adapted to a particular period or, one
might say, was best suited to that section of humanity occupied
with such thoughts.

During the first centuries that followed the advent of Christianity into world history, we realize in connection with a certain trend of ideas and spiritual tendency that has been called
gnosis [a term denoting a higher spiritual wisdom claimed by the
Gnostics] that grand and mighty concepts were formed with
regard to the being whom we term the Christ. We find, however, that the universal acceptance of these exalted gnostic conceptions continued for only a relatively short period compared
with that idea of the Christ, which was generally approved and
spread among the people and later became the essence of the
church movement. It will be enlightening to consider briefly
those lofty Christ concepts that evolved in the form of gnostic

conceptions during the first centuries of the Christian era—
not, be it understood, because spiritual science would seek to
cloak those ideas it has to put forward with regard to the Christ
beneath a mantle of gnostic notions; such an assertion could be
made only by those who, because of the immaturity of their
development in the field of spiritual science, are wholly incapable of truly differentiating between the nature of the various
events and conditions met with in spiritual life.

In many ways the concepts of the spiritual science of today,
which will be recapitulated in this lecture, extend far beyond the
ancient gnosis of those early Christian times, but this very fact
makes it the more interesting that we should at least touch upon
these old spiritual conceptions. There are many different points
of view in connection with this bygone higher wisdom and various degrees of light and shade in that olden spiritual trend of
thought, and we will draw attention to one of its most important aspects, which harmonizes best with the teachings of spiritual science in our time. During the first few centuries of the
Christian era, this ancient gnosis put forward the most profound ideas concerning the Christ-being—momentous indeed
in relation to the enlightenment that came with the dawn of
Christianity. This higher spiritual wisdom maintained that the
Christ-being was eternal and not alone associated and concerned with the evolution and development of humanity but
with the surrounding world of the cosmos taken in its entirety.

When considering the question of the origin of the human
being, we found that we were taken back to a form of humanity that floated or hovered, as it were, entirely in spiritual
heights and was not yet familiar with or embodied in an outer
material covering. We have seen that during the process of the
earth's evolution, humanity, starting from a purely spiritual

state, gradually changed into that of a lower and denser form we now call the human being and that owing to the materialistic outlook of the present theory of evolution, which merely follows human earthly history backward, their beginning has been traced to external animal forms. Spiritual science, on the other hand, leads us directly to previous states that approach nearer and nearer to the immaterial soul and finally points definitely to a spiritual origin.

The old gnosis sought the Christ-being in that region in which human beings had hovered before they assumed material existence and where they felt themselves surrounded only by spiritual life and spiritual reality. If we understand this ancient gnosis rightly, we must look upon it from the gnostic point of view, that when human beings had so far developed as to have reached a point when their etheric body should be enclosed within a material covering so that they might take part in the general course of physical evolution, there remained behind in the purely spiritual realms what might be termed a bygone companion of the human being, or "alter ego," in the form of an element of the Christ-being, which did not descend into the physical world. Further, according to this conception, humankind was destined to undergo a process of continued development in the material plane, and it was their mission to show evidence of achievement and progress. Hence, according to the gnosis, this Christ element continues to dwell in the spiritual realms while humanity undergoes a period of material evolution, so that during the whole time of the human being's earthly history the Christ-being is not to be sought in that region to which the human being is related as a physical perceptual entity but only in the realms of pure spirit.

The particular period that we call the birth of Christianity the ancient gnosis considered of special import in the evolution of humanity on the earth. It was regarded as that glorious moment when the Christ-being entered the physical perceptual world to give an impulse to spiritual activity, for humans had retarded the soul's development after they had descended to the material plane. The gnosis looked upon the primeval human during the very beginning of evolution as a spiritual being bound to a world in which the Christ was *then* active, and it considered that Christ *again* descended upon our earth, where for a long period of time humanity had been undergoing material evolution, at that particular period from which we now reckon our time.

The question now arises, How did the ancient wisdom actually look upon this descent of a purely spiritual being into the evolution of humanity? It was regarded in the following manner: According to the gnosis, an especially highly developed human individuality, to whom historical research has given the name of Jesus of Nazareth, had achieved such exceptional spiritual maturity that at a particular period definite soul conditions had come about by virtue of which this singular personality had the power to absorb certain divine qualities and wisdom from the spirit world, which up to then no human could acquire. From this time on, so the gnosis states, the soul of this specially selected personality felt itself sufficiently advanced to surrender to the indwelling of that divine being who up to that moment had had no part in the actual progress and development of humanity—namely, the Christ. The event that took place on the banks of the Jordan when Jesus of Nazareth was baptized by John, and which is recorded in the Bible (Mark I:9–11), was regarded by this ancient gnosis as a manifestation of the entering of the Christ-being into the course of human evolution. The gnosis further declared that some very singular spiritual condition had been engendered with regard to Jesus through this sacred baptism, which event we may consider as wholly symbolic or otherwise.

We can obtain an idea of what underlies this gnostic concept if we pursue a line of thought somewhat as follows: We begin with a realization of the fact that if we carefully observe the lives of other people, using those methods of thought that lead us to the very depth of the soul and not the superficial mode so typical of our time, we shall often find in the experience of such persons moments fraught with epoch-making events, when they feel that they stand at a turning point in their lives. A situation of this nature may arise through some deep-lying sorrow or other trial of earthly origin. Then indeed they may say, "That which has now befallen me differs from all my previous experiences, for it causes me to look upon myself as a person transformed." It is certain that in the case of many people there occurs at times something in the nature of a crisis, such as might be described as an awakening and renewing of special and distinctive forces of soul life.

If we imagine an experience of this kind as representing in a very imperfect and elementary manner an inner event similar to that which the gnosis regarded as having taken place at the time of the baptism of Jesus in Jordan (Mark 1:9), we can then readily conceive an entirely different form of happening hitherto unknown in connection with human existence and quite unlike any that may break in upon human beings' souls and is born merely of earthly trials and vicissitudes. The divine power and supreme spiritual quality that flamed up in the soul of Jesus of Nazareth manifested in wholly new indwelling attributes; from them arose a godlike inner life, shedding fresh

light upon all forms of human culture enlivened by its example. It was the divine essence that entered into the innermost
being of Jesus of Nazareth—that glorious and most Holy
Spirit creating in him a newborn life—that the ancient gnosis
termed THE CHRIST.

The gnosis clearly realized that through the Christ there had
come to humanity something in the nature of a new impulse,
an impulse differing utterly from any that had been before. For
all the godlike stimulating power that was brought forth and
unfolded in Jesus during the three years subsequent to his baptism by John was such as had never up to that time found a
place in the evolution of humanity. The gnosis states quite definitely that we must not consider a particular man [Jesus of
Nazareth] as the Christ [as is oftentimes done] but that we
must realize and look for the Christ in the divine spirit manifested IN Jesus through those sublime and singular qualities
that were latent within his innermost being.

We have characterized this ancient spiritual wisdom concerning the Christ in this way so that it it is easy to comprehend. In the example previously cited of a special turning
point occurring in the life of a human soul, we have an
instance at least in some ways analogous to the Christ event
expressed in its most elementary form. It is especially difficult
for humanity in these modern times to realize that circumstances of fundamental historic significance are directly connected with this outstanding incident and which are of such
momentous import as to form what might be termed the true
center of human evolution. When we compare this gnostic
concept with various statements of spiritual science brought
to your notice during these lectures, we find that no matter
how we regard the facts, it not only has a grand and glorious

conception of the Christ-being but also evinces an exalted idea of the inner being of humanity, for it regards the human being as being involved in an impulse coming directly from the spiritual realms and brought to bear upon the actual course of humanity's historic growth and development. It is therefore not to be wondered at that this ancient gnostic conception was unpopular. Anyone who has obtained even a slight insight into the circumstances connected with the progress of humanity during the early centuries of the Christian era onward, the existing state of the human soul, and the various conditions of social life at different periods must at once admit that such concepts imply a loftiness of sentiment that was certainly not destined to find favor among the people. To appreciate this point, we have only to consider the spiritual life of the present day.

Whenever conversation turns upon any idea similar in character to this ancient higher spiritual wisdom, the majority of people at once say, "That is all an abstraction, a purely visionary notion—what we want is reality, something that directly affects our actual material life." Thus it is that even in our time humanity for the most part regards the old gnostic conception, as outlined here, merely in the light of a wholly abstract impression. Humanity is still far from experiencing the feeling of greater satisfaction that comes of spiritual thought and realizing how much more true is the substantiality of all that underlies those spiritual concepts to which we may raise ourselves than is that of the things most people regard as perceptual, concrete, and having absolute reality. If it were otherwise, we would not find, as is the case in the arts and professions, that people are always urged toward what may be touched and seen, while all that is of the spirit and calls for inner upliftment of the soul for its apprehension is pushed aside and regarded as abstract and visionary.

It is not possible in a few words to explain just how the popular conception of the Christ-being evolved in the minds of the people. But it may be said that an echo of the true Christ concept, which pictures a divine being incarnate and abiding in the man Jesus of Nazareth, has lived on through the centuries side by side with that simple idea of Jesus, which looks upon him as born in a marvelous manner and as ever approaching humanity with divine tenderness and love, a theme developed even in the story of his childhood. In this concept we find Jesus of Nazareth hailed by humanity as its loving Savior. It is in that holy sense and feeling evoked by the deeds of this beloved Redeemer that we find a dim echo of the ancient gnostic Christ concept. During the whole course of what we might call the external history of Jesus, there is found an upturned vision that realized the presence of a great secret truth, an awe-inspiring mystery, which even as Jesus walked the earth endowed his personality with superhuman attributes. This superhuman quality has been termed the Christ. Moreover, we find that as time went on, humanity became less and less capable of understanding that bold concept, the gnostic Christ, and this ever-increasing inability of comprehension has continued up to the present day.

Already in the Middle Ages we note that science dared to reason only concerning that which is external and directly apparent to the senses or about those things it conceived as lying beyond our sense perception in a kind of world governed by natural laws. It did not feel itself called upon to probe into those factors and influences that have entered into and played their respective parts in human evolution in the form of noble and uplifting spiritual impulses. Thus it was that in the Middle

Ages, questions concerning the origin and evolution of humanity in which the Christ impulse made itself felt became solely objects of belief. This spiritual faith, however, continued among the people from that time side by side with all that was regarded as science and absolute knowledge but which took heed only of the lower order of cosmic matters and events.

At this point it is of interest to note that from the sixteenth century onward, this twofold method of thought has more and more tended toward a crisis and for the reason that humanity was always prone to direct and confine their powers of cognition to the perceptual world alone and to assign all matters of spiritual origin and dependent upon spiritual progress and evolution to the category of mere dogma.

We cannot, however, enter upon this subject at the present time, for it is more essential that I now draw your attention to the fact that in the nineteenth century the course of development led humankind to a point where, one might say, all true conception of the Christ was wholly lost, at least to a very large proportion of the people. Nevertheless, we must admit that among a small section of the community the ancient gnostic concepts lived on and were yet further developed after a manner that we might regard as bringing about a deeper insight into the Christ impulse. In the case of the majority, even among the scientific theological circles, there was a general renunciation of the true Christ concept. An attempt was made to center all in the personality of Jesus of Nazareth and to look upon him as one possessed of singular attributes and especially chosen because of his profound and all-embracing comprehension of the laws and conditions of human evolution and the divine inner nature of humanity—but even so to be considered a *man*, though a man transcendent in all things. Thus it came about that in those days, in place of the old Christology, there grew up what might be called a mere Jesus life research. The results of this mode of thought and study became more and more incredible when considered in the light of all those divine qualities that dwelled within the being of the chosen one, Jesus of Nazareth. According to these investigations, Jesus was to be regarded as one specifically selected as endowed with supreme and unique spiritual attributes but nevertheless possessed of human individuality.

The crowning point in this class of conception is reached in such works as that entitled *What Is Christianity*, by Adolf Harnack,[17] and other similar attempts in the direction of what we have termed Jesus life research and which have appeared in many and varied forms. For the present, however, it is necessary only to draw attention to the results obtained from deep and earnest study along these lines; since this subject is the most modern of any with which we are concerned, we can do so very briefly. We would say that the methods employed during the nineteenth century to authenticate historically those events that occurred at the beginning of the Christian era have led to no actual positive conclusions.

It would take us much too far to enter into any kind of detail respecting this particular trend of thought, but anyone who will make a careful investigation into the results achieved in modern times in this connection will know that an endeavor

---

17. *Das Wesen des Christentums* (1903), Harnack's most popularly influential work. Adolf von Harnack (1851-1930) was one of the foremost liberal German theologians of the late nineteenth-early twentieth century. From his extensive studies of early Christianity and Christian dogma he claimed that their development was a strictly historical process that could be understood through historical-critical method alone.

has been made to apply the ordinary methods of external research to prove that the personality of Jesus of Nazareth actually lived at the beginning of our Christian spiritual life. This attempt to demonstrate the existence of Jesus by such historical means as may be applied in other cases has led merely to the following admission: It is impossible to confirm the personality of Jesus of Nazareth by external material methods. It by no means follows that the negative assumption, which claims that Jesus never lived, is thereby proved. These material investigations have simply shown that we cannot employ the same historical means to verify the life of Jesus of Nazareth as may be used to demonstrate the existence of Aristotle, Socrates, or Alexander the Great. But that is not all—lately, this field of inquiry has led to serious difficulties experienced in quite another direction.

It is only necessary to refer to such works as those by William Benjamin Smith, published by Diederich of Leipzig,[18] to realize that the result of painstaking and exact research into biblical and other documentary records relating to Christianity has again revealed the fact that [in many instances] these venerable documents cannot be referring to those matters to which, during the greater part of the nineteenth century, it was generally supposed they had reference. A special attempt was made to reconstruct the life of Jesus of Nazareth from the results of philological investigations into these ancient chronicles, but in the end it was found that in the very writings themselves there was evidence of an underlying significance of quite a different nature from that which appeared upon the surface. It became apparent that despite every effort to picture the life of Jesus by

---

18. See, for example, *Ecce Deus: Studies of Primitive Christianity*, London, 1912.

employing the most carefully chosen and exact methods, the biblical records—those Christian documents wherein humanity feels itself upon a firm and truly Christian foundation—hardly mention Jesus of Nazareth as a human being.

External science is thus driven to the following statement: "The ancient records scarcely ever allude to Jesus of Nazareth as a man; they refer to Him as a God." Again there is this remarkable anomalous assertion: "It is an error to believe that any proof may be found in the original Christian documents of the existence of Jesus of Nazareth as an actual human personality. Rather do we come to the conviction that what the evangelical and other olden sacred writings state is that in the very beginning of the Christian era was a deity; only when we recognize this fact does all that is written in these aged chronicles become of true significance and import."

Now is not this all very extraordinary? According to the investigations of our period, when we allude to Jesus of Nazareth, we must speak of a deity, but this same period and same line of research admits of no reality in this god or purely spiritual being. How, then, does present-day science regard the Christ? He is looked upon as a visionary creation, a mere ideal concept that insinuated itself into the history of humanity and was called into being by a folk fantasy born of mental impulse. According to the latest investigations in this field, the Christ is to be regarded not as a reality but as a kind of imaginary god. To put it plainly, we would say that modern scientific research is brought face to face with something for which it has absolutely no use. What can it do with a god in whom it has no faith? External science has merely proved that the Bible records speak of a deity, but it knows of nothing else to do with this deity than to ascribe to him a place in the category of visionary concepts.

We will now compare the attitude of external science, as characterized here, with what spiritual science has to say upon the matter. At this point I should like to mention a book entitled *Christianity as Mystical Fact*, of which I am the author. The fundamental idea underlying this work has been but little understood. I have therefore endeavored to set forth its object more clearly in a preface to the second edition. My intention was to show that the history of humanity—world history—is not complete in that picture we can generally obtain from external history and external documents, for this reason: Throughout all human evolution spiritual impulses are at work, spiritual factors are present, and these we must attribute to the agency of spiritual beings. If with this concept we compare the whole nature and method of the historic world conception put forward by Leopold von Ranke and others, we can only say that the highest point the science of history has yet reached is that it actually speaks of *historical ideas* as if they were subject to the intrusion of abstract impressions coming from outside during the course of human evolution and the development of nations and of peoples. That is the utmost extent of general belief in this direction. But "ideas" are not what historians consider them to be and do not develop force and exhibit power. The whole process of human evolution would be lifeless and spiritless if it proceeded merely historically and if it were not that those ideas that enter into the souls of human beings are the expression of invisible and supersensible impulses, which rule and govern the whole of human growth and development. Behind all that is revealed in this external progression, there still remains something that can be unveiled only by those supersensible means at the disposal of spiritual science, where the methods are applicable to things beyond the powers of our sense perception. Attention has already been drawn to this subject in a previous lecture, and we shall again refer to it at a future date.

I could demonstrate to you how the Christ impulse entered historically into the evolution of humanity in such a way that it proved itself to be an actual continuation of the self-same influence that played its part in the spiritual development of humankind in the old days of the ancient mysteries, the actual nature of which is but little understood. A true comprehension of all that was accomplished in pre-Christian times by the old mysteries in connection with the laying down of spiritual foundations for the development of nations and of peoples can arise only when, through the methods of modern spiritual science, humanity has gained an understanding of that particular form of development through which the soul is transformed into an instrument capable of apprehending that spirit world that lies behind all things material and perceptual. In these lectures I have many times referred to transformations of this character.

We now know that human beings, who in these days are in a sense confined and interested only in the immediate experiences of their intimate soul lives, may truly raise themselves above their present state and assume a more perfect form of soul being, which can live in the spirit world even as the human counterpart lives in the physical world. Through the study of history in the light of spiritual science, we learn that the possibility of raising the soul being to spiritual heights through a process of purely intimate individual soul development has come about gradually during the evolution of humanity and was not known in primeval times. Whereas the soul may now through its own effort and measures rise freely and, while still possessed of its individual quality, acquire the power of spiritual discernment, in pre-Christian times such was not the case. For the soul was then dependent upon an impulse born of certain modes and procedures that were a part of the rites performed in the sanctuaries of the Mysteries.

In *Christianity as Mystical Fact*, I have presented a somewhat detailed account of those ancient rites conducted by the priests in connection with the soul. These ceremonies took place in the various temples of the Mysteries, as they were then considered to be but which in this lecture we will regard more as temples assigned to spiritual instruction. What actually took place in these sanctuaries may be briefly outlined as follows: By means of certain methods and observances, the soul was freed from its bodily covering, and it was made possible for it to remain for a time in a condition similar to, though in many ways differing from, the ordinary sleep state.

When we consider the sleep state in the light of spiritual science, we see that while the human frame remains quiescent and sleeping, the actual center of the human etheric being is situated outside the recumbent figure and that during such state the power of the true inner essence of this etheric nucleus is so low that unconsciousness supervenes and the nucleus becomes, as it were, enveloped in darkness. The methods employed during these ancient mystic rites in order to affect the human soul were as follows: Through the influence of certain advanced personalities, who had themselves passed through similar mystical initiation, a species of sleep state was first induced. This was of such nature that the inner forces of the soul were thereby strengthened and intensified. When a certain stage was reached, the soul left the body, which was then in a condition of death-like sleep, and for a time entered upon a psychic existence—a kind of sleep life, during which it could look upon the spirit world with full consciousness. While this sleep life continued, the soul was able to realize its true position as an inhabitant of the spiritual realms. When, in due course, the soul was brought back once again to ordinary mundane conditions, there came to it recollections of all those things it had observed and experienced while freed from the body. It was then that it could [while active within the human form] come before the people and stand forth as a prophet, bringing to them proofs of the existence of a spirit world and of an eternal life to come. In those olden days it was in the manner indicated here that the soul was enabled to take part in the life of the spiritual realms. In the Mysteries were found the canons to which it must submit and for a long period, in order that the supreme spiritual leaders in the ancient Mystery sanctuaries might bring about the final consummation of the soul's desire.

We will now ask this question: Whence came those ancient standards of human conduct that have been passed on by peoples spread throughout the world during the course of human evolution and those flashes of spiritual enlightenment proclaiming our godlike origin and the eternity of the soul? The answer comes through spiritual science; from it we learn that this old wisdom originated with those who had themselves undergone initiation after the manner we have outlined. There is a reflection of these primeval moral precedents manifested in strange and curious fashion in connection with myths and legends and various graphic portrayals of the past. In these very fables we find depicted many of the same experiences that came as if in a living dream to the initiates in the Mystery sanctuaries. Indeed, we first begin to understand mythology rightly when we regard the forms and figures there presented as pictorial representations of things that appeared to the spiritual vision of the initiates during the time of their participation in the secret rites. If we would establish a relation between the mythological conceptions of long-ago times and the religious teachings of an earlier age, we must hark back to the ancient Mysteries and ponder all that lay concealed therein, deeply hidden from a profane external world. These Mysteries were revealed to those alone who, through severe trials and unswerving observance of that secrecy and restraint imposed upon all, had truly fitted themselves to take part in the dark ceremonies of initiation. We cannot, however, at this point enter into the actual circumstances that led to the close veiling of the mystic rites performed in that remote, gray past. When we turn our gaze backward and follow the course of spiritual development in pre-Christian times, however, we realize that it was always in the dim obscurity enshrouding the inscrutable observances of that bygone age that the human soul unfolded and was strengthened.

The souls of human beings were not so fully developed in the past that they could of themselves and through their own efforts rise upward and enter the realms of the spirit, while remaining merely dependent upon their immediate powers and unaided by the ministrations of the temple priests. In *Christianity as Mystical Fact* I have pointed out that even while external history ran its course, a change was taking place; it has there been my object to show how the whole plan and design underlying human evolution was such that when the turning point was reached that marked the birth of Christianity, humankind was already prepared to enter upon a new era. This change had come about because of all that human beings had experienced and absorbed through repeated reincarnations and through knowledge gained from initiates concerning the spirit world. From then on, they would have the power of upliftment to spiritual heights within their own innermost soul, which could henceforth rise of its own effort, free from all external influence and unaided by those means it was the custom to employ in the bygone days of the Mysteries.

According to the views we now hold, the most outstanding event that came to pass in Palestine in connection with the spiritual progress of humanity was the final perfecting of the soul, so that it should be fitted for what we might call self-initiation. This ultimate consummation had been approached gradually, and the necessary preparation had extended over possibly hundreds of years; the end came just about at the very time when that special turning point was reached which marked the beginning of the Christian era. The soul was then so far perfected that it was ready for self-initiation, during which it would be merely guided by those having knowledge of the true path and of the trials that must be endured. Henceforth self-initiation might be achieved without external aid rendered by temple priests or by leaders having an understanding of the Mysteries. Furthermore, through the founding of Christianity, all those other rites and observances that were performed time and time again in the innermost sanctuaries of the temples, memories of which are still preserved in legends, myths, and mythologies connected with folklore, are found to have a place in that grand plan that underlies the world's history.

If we would indeed understand the Gospels, we should ask ourselves the following question: What experiences were essential to a candidate for initiation in the days of the ancient Persians or Egyptians, who desired so to uplift their souls that they might gaze directly upon the spirit world? Injunctions concerning such matters were clearly set forth and formed the basis of what we might term a ritual of initiation. These commands and

instructions covered a time extending from a certain event designated by some as the baptism and by others as the temptation
up to that moment when the soul was led forth and blessed with
a true discernment of the spiritual realms. When we compare
such initiation rituals with the most important statements contained in the Gospels, then (as I have shown in *Christianity as
Mystical Fact*) we find that in the Gospels there appear once again
detailed narratives concerning ancient initiation ceremonies—
but here the descriptions have reference to that great outstanding historical character Jesus of Nazareth. It further becomes
clear that whereas in previous times an initiation candidate was
raised to spiritual heights in the seclusion of the temples of the
Mysteries, Jesus of Nazareth, because of the course history had
taken, was already so far advanced that he not only remembered
his experiences in the spirit world and thus brought enlightenment to humanity but also became unified in spirit with one to
whom no earthly being had as yet become united—the
Christ-being. Thus we find a great similarity between the
descriptions of the course of the ancient forms of initiation and
the narrative of the spiritual development of Jesus of Nazareth
up to that moment when the Christ entered into his soul and
during the following three years, when he drew inspiration and
wisdom from this divine source.

In the accounts that tell us of all the trials and experiences
Jesus of Nazareth underwent in those days, we find the events
connected with his initiation clearly marked by the magnitude
and godlike nature of the spiritual facts that underlie the historical descriptions. This is especially noticeable in the Gospel
of John. While in previous times countless aspirants had taken
part in the sacred rites, they had advanced only to that point
when they could testify as follows: "The spiritual world is a

reality, and to such a world does the human soul belong." But when it came to pass that Jesus was himself initiated, he became actually unified and at one with the most significant and outstanding of all spiritual beings ever remembered by former initiates; it was toward this supreme initiation that the ordered plan underlying all ancient forms and ceremonies had its trend.

Even though what we may term the human being's deepest life center has always been near at hand, the awareness of this life center had not up to the time of that great happening really penetrated into the consciousness of humanity. It was ordained that through the Mystery of Golgotha human beings' eyes should be opened and a new era be entered upon, in which it would be realized that in the life center, the Ego, there manifests an element common to both the individual human being and the entire cosmos. Thus do we behold the Mystery of Golgotha emerging from those secrets hidden in the dark Mysteries of the past to take its place in that grand design so fundamental to the world's history. As long as human beings refuse to believe that in a certain locality and at a definite time Jesus of Nazareth was blessed with divine initiation and imbued with the spirit of the Christ in such manner that this almighty influence could stream forth and act as an impulse upon all future generations—just so long will they remain unable to realize the true import and meaning of the Christ impulse in its relation to the evolution of humanity. When, through the study of the basic principles of spiritual science, the reality of great spiritual events such as we have portrayed is admitted, then will first dawn a true comprehension of all that has come to human evolution through the advent of the Christ impulse. Then we shall no longer degrade the Gospels by discovering in them four separate rituals of initiation in which matters and circumstances concerning Jesus of Nazareth are hidden away and mysteriously concealed. When we come to understand these things rightly, we will realize that everything that followed as a result of the event in Palestine held a deep significance for all later periods of human evolution.

 If we would know in what manner that great and vital change wrought in the world's history by the coming of the Christ impulse is regarded when viewed in the light of spiritual science, then we must first realize that the human being consists of a physical body, an etheric or life body, and an astral body; deep within and underlying all is the Ego—that true "I" which continues from incarnation to incarnation.[19] An awareness of the presence of this ultimate center of life broke in upon human consciousness last of all, such that in pre-Christian times humans had no thought of its existence. Even as the physical body is directly united and in contact with the physical world and the astral body with the astral world, so is the human being's deepest life center, the Ego born of that spirit world that passes the human being's uttermost understanding. Hence, the great message that Christianity and the Christ impulse brought to humankind may be thus expressed: Seek not the deity and the godlike primordial principle in the astral body but in the human being's innermost being, for there abides the true Ego.

Previous to the advent of Christianity people would exclaim, "My soul is indeed rooted in the divine. It is the divine quality alone that can extend the vision and bring to me true enlightenment [through the powers of those who have a deeper knowledge of spiritual matters]." But now people are learning to say,

---

19. See the lecture on Moses; footnote to p. 121.

"If you would truly know where you can unveil the profoundest depths of all that is divine and active throughout the world, look within your Ego, for therein lies the channel through which comes to you the Word of God. His voice will break in upon your conscious state if you rightly understand that because of the Mystery of Golgotha the powers that are of God have entered into humanity and if thou will realize that then indeed was a glorious initiation truly consummated—to stand forth as a grand historical event. But especially does God speak to you if you exalt yourself and make your soul an instrument able and fitted to apprehend that which is of the spiritual realms."

Before that supreme act came to pass at Golgotha, the way of those who would enter upon the life of the spirit lay through the deep mysteries of the temple sanctuaries. The actual awakening of the divine consciousness that speaks through the Ego is the very essence of the Christ impulse, and the growth and development of the ancient initiation principle paved the way and made it possible for this great impulse to come to humanity. During the whole future course of evolution, because of the Mystery of Golgotha, there will enter into human souls an ever-increasing clarity of understanding and discernment of the divine spirit to which humanity is so truly united—that same Holy Spirit which even now speaks through the Ego when humanity has indeed freed itself from all earthly conditions and circumstances.

He who can understand the Gospels from this point of view will realize the wonderful evidence of racial development and preparation for those coming events brought about in the past by the powers of the spirit world. It will be apparent that throughout the ancient Hebrew evolution, humankind was being made ready to hear the voice that would later speak through the deep centre of the human being, the Ego-center, even as the spirit of the old Hebrew race spoke to Judaism. But the people of other nations had heard no such voice, for they were conscious of the divine spirit only as it held converse with the soul in the case of those who were truly initiated.

It had become clear to Judaism that the evolution of humankind is a continuous process of development and progress and that deep within the human Ego there dwell those mystic forces that appertain to the human being's innermost being. Hence the Jew became conscious of this thought: "When as an isolated personality, a part of the ancient Hebrew race, I look back upon the course of human evolution from the time of Abraham and realize that supreme deity who has ruled over all things from generation to generation, there comes over me a vague indefinable feeling that everything divine and of that holy spiritual power that has fashioned the individual qualities of humankind lives in me." In this way the individual members of the old Hebrew race felt that they were united and at one with Abraham, their father. But Christianity definitely states that all such thoughts and conceptions concerning the godlike qualities in the human being are lacking completeness and fail to picture human beings in their most perfect form, even though they believe within themselves that "I AM THAT I AM." A true realization of those divine attributes and forces active deep within humanity can come only when there is a clear apprehension of those things that are of the spirit and lie beyond all human generations.

Therefore, if we would give the preceding words their fuller and truer meaning, we should say: "Before Abraham, was the I AM." This implies that the human Ego is eternal and that in the beginning was the same godlike element that has continued throughout all generations and will be for evermore. To this the Hebrew would add: "Look not upon that which fades away and is of human material being, but regard only the divine essence that has lived and flowed in the blood of all descendants of Abraham, who was indeed our father. See to it that you know and discern this Holy Spirit in each one of God's children. But seek it not in the bond that unites brother and sister but in that which abides in each one of you and comes to light when human beings, in solitude, know themselves in their innermost soul and cry out, 'I AM.'"

Christ Jesus uttered words of similar intent and which we must interpret in like manner. With one modification they are as follows: "If any *man* come to me, and forsaketh ["hate" in Luke 14:26] not his father, and mother, and wife, and children, and brethren, and sisters, yea, and his own life also, he cannot be my disciple."[20] We must not regard the significance of this passage as in any way conflicting with the just claims of relationship and child love but rather as indicating that the Christ had brought into the world the principle of divine spirit that all human beings, *because they are human beings,* may find if they only seek steadfastly in the very center of their being. It was because of this transcendent deed that afterward humankind would enter into closer and closer contact with the very heart of Christianity. Then would this most sacred principle rise up supreme and, while overcoming all diversity and error, bring about the realization of that universal quality that all may discern who look deep within.

---

20. What is here implied is that the longing to be at one with the Christ spirit that came into the world through Jesus of Nazareth should be so intense that each of his disciples must be ready to sacrifice all ties of human love so that he may devote his life and being to the absolute service of THE CHRIST who manifests within. Judging from the context, the word "Hate" found in Luke 14:26 would appear to be of doubtful origin.

The old gods were ethnic gods, clan gods, and were connected to certain tribal characteristics. Something of the same nature may be ascribed to Hinduism, and even somewhat to Buddhism. But the God who stands revealed through Christianity is one who will raise humankind above all human discord and divergence and lead them on to that which they truly are because they are indeed human beings. Those who would gain knowledge of the fundamental character of the Christian doctrine must necessarily regard those spiritual powers and impulses that have guided supreme events in world history as *realities*. [They cannot aver that all was begotten of mere chance actions and purely human mental activity.] They must break away from previous concepts of what is basic and of primary historic import, for happenings that have long been so regarded in reality lie upon the surface of the world's actual growth. Underlying and controlling all human progress and development are beings far above humans' normal powers of sense perception who are just as real as is the animal and the human being in our material world. Supreme and preeminent among those spirit mentors who govern and direct the growth and development of humanity is THE CHRIST—that Christ, who, according to the ancient gnosis, was active in the body of Jesus of Nazareth for a period of three years.

Once again do we realize that spiritual science has attained to a concept and understanding that enables it to throw light upon matters that have already claimed the attention of external science. Science has been forced to admit that [with respect to the Christ] we are not merely concerned with a man but with a divine being who, while he ruled and gave guidance, must in a certain sense be considered as active within the man Jesus. Here, however, we come upon a situation with which external science is unable to cope. Spiritual science, on the other hand, leads us to the direct contemplation of beings thus acted upon and made subservient to divine spiritual powers in the manner indicated and regards such states as actually having occurred. Thus it can approach this sphere of modern investigation in a proper and logical manner. An amazing feature of twentieth-century spiritual development will be that external science will recognize and acknowledge that the concepts of the nineteenth century were in error, insofar as an attempt was then made to reduce the life of *Christ* Jesus to a life of Jesus of Nazareth only. Further it will be found that the final result of all research in this field will prove that in *Christ* Jesus we are concerned with a god; when any science proclaims this truth, it is a sign that it has begun to follow the true path. Spiritual science would merely add that if humankind once admits the truth of this statement, it may go forward assured that it is upon a certain and absolute foundation. The concept expressed in this assertion is certainly in direct opposition to that material monistic cosmic conception formed in modern times.

In the two lectures to which I have already referred, "The Origin of the Human Being" and "The Origin of the Animal Kingdom," we have seen that spiritual science was in complete accord with the actual facts brought to light by external science. We would here say that in the matter we are now considering spiritual science is again disposed to associate itself with the results of conscientious scientific research; where there is doubt and divergence, it will be found that external science falls short of that goal that may be reached through the methods of spiritual science. Today human beings regard human life and human understanding, as they appear to them in the physical world, as if they were irreconcilable with a closely associated and actual outer spiritual realm. They further believe that, at the most, human beings' greatest fault can lie only in forming wrong conceptions of the material world or in doing something looked upon as detrimental or malicious and that does not conform with outer and apparent progress.

It is the custom at the present time, in connection with the existing cosmic concept, to seek the origin of phenomena only in that which is close at hand; it has become more and more clear the further human beings penetrate into spiritual life that a point has been reached with regard to this method where a complete change in ideas has become necessary. Both natural science and history have come to a stage where there is definite scepticism concerning all spiritual matters, and these external sciences are now employed merely in collecting and associating outer perceptual facts, wholly regardless of that underlying spiritual reality that may be apprehended in all phenomena capable of sense perception. One might almost say that our present period has reached a point where scientific thought must be reversed and assume a directly opposite attitude. The soul, through its constant inner striving, will in the end lead ultramaterialism and ultramaterialistic monism to adopt a concept that as yet has played but a small part in human ideas concerning the cosmos. In future investigations into the origin of things, there will enter thoughts and ideas so far not generally accepted.

In my two works *The Philosophy of Spiritual Activity*[21] and *Truth and Science*,[22] I have explained that human beings have been com-

21. This work, originally called by Steiner *Die Philosophie der Freiheit* (*The Philosophy of Freedom*), is volume 4 in The Collected Works of Rudolf Steiner (CW). It has also been published as *The Philosophy of Spiritual Activity* and *Intuitive Thinking as a Spiritual Path* (Anthroposophic Press, 1995).
22. CW 3.

pelled to assume that the position in which they find themselves relative to the world is not their true position and that they must first undergo a development of inner life so that they may recognize reality in natural phenomena, in order to be able to place themselves in a just and ethical relation to such phenomena. Moreover, in the mind of human beings there must dawn a clear understanding of the fundamental idea of redemption in addition to mere apprehension of causative factors in life. It will be a task of the twentieth century to gain general acceptance of the concepts pertaining to redemption, deliverance, and reincarnation among the external sciences. The position that human beings have assumed as expert and judge of the world does not represent reality, for they can arrive at true concepts only after they have freed themselves from their present false ideas, risen to a higher standard of thought, and overcome those barriers that cause them to view all things in distorted and unreal form—such a consummation would be perceptive redemption.

Moral redemption comes about when human beings feel that the position they occupy in their relation to the world is not their true standing and when they realize that they must seek a path leading over those obstacles that tower above them, blocking the way to all things pertaining to their true place in life. Concepts of the soul's rebirth upon a higher plane will yet be evolved from the wonders that come to light through the investigations of natural science and the results of historical research. Human beings will then know, if they picture the world as in a photographic image and conjure forth a vision of the scientific and historic progress of humankind, that this vision does not represent the material world alone, for underlying all human advancement there is clear evidence of a mighty spiritual plan of earnest training and development. They will no longer believe that the world as depicted by science is a mere physical creation, for they will realize that God's laws are always operative in such a manner as to bring about his gradual unfoldment.

If only natural science would extend its sphere of action beyond a mere portrayal of the perceptual world and rightly educate humankind, so that the human soul might break away from a position that is untenable and rise to a state that would permit its rebirth into a more exalted life—and if human beings could know how glorious would then be the freedom from that restraint that hinders upward progress—they would indeed have developed within themselves those things fundamental to a true world concept of the Christ impulse. They would realize that they have power to look back into the gray mists of the past to a period to which we have often referred, when their true being dwelled in a purely spiritual realm, later to descend into the material world that they might there, of their own effort, further their growth and advancement. Then would humankind understand the reason why it became imperative, at a certain definite period in earthly progress, that a complete change of thought, a reversal of ideas, be brought about. They would know that it was in order that all might be empowered to tear themselves away from those false, deceptive, material concepts that have entered so deeply into human consciousness. It is the Christ impulse that has checked human beings' fall and has saved humanity from being utterly immersed in those things that are only of the material world [and have neither value nor reality].

With respect to the evolution of humanity, the Christ is to be regarded objectively as the [divine principle] that is the source of our experience of a sacred power and quality entering the soul when reborn and freed of all those primal transgressive tendencies that seek to find expression when the human being is associated with external earthly progress. It is this most holy essence, flowing in upon the world, that is indeed the manifestation we know as the Christ.

If the twentieth century would regard the glorious realities of the human being's inner life in a serious light, it would understand the Christ event and no more be in conflict with the concept and truth of those happenings that take place during the soul's rebirth into a higher sphere. Spiritual science would then prove that the same actual principles underlie all historic progress and development as are obtained in the case of external natural phenomena and occurrences. With regard to human beings' ideas concerning the cosmos, they have fallen into the very error that finds expression in the words of Schopenhauer "The world is my own conception." This statement implies that we are surrounded by a universe of color, sound, and so forth that is dependent entirely upon the action of the eye and other sense organs for its being. But if we seek to comprehend the world in its totality, it is not true to say, "All color has existence only by virtue of the physical constitution of the eye." For the organ of sight would not be there if the light had not first conjured it into being. If, on the one hand, it is true that the sensation of light is determined by the eye's structure, it is equally true, on the other hand, that the eye has been created by the light through the sun's action. Both of these truths must therefore be involved in one incomprehensible reality. Thus do we realize the truth underlying Goethe's words, when he says, "The eye must thank the light for its being."

From animal matter the light has brought forth a corresponding instrument suitable to receive its impressions. Thus has the eye formed itself in the light, so that it could be sensible to its touch and so that the illumination which is within could meet and blend with the rays coming from the outer world. Even as the eye has been fashioned through the light's action and apprehension of the latter comes through the agency of this organ of vision, so was the fulfilment of the human being's inner Christ experience and rebirth of soul brought about by that supreme Christ event—the Mystery of Golgotha. Spiritual science tells us that before the advent of the Christ impulse, such inner experience could occur only under the stimulus of an external influence created through the agency of the Mysteries and not, as is now the case, through a form of self-initiation induced within the human being's very being.

The twentieth century will see the dawn of those conditions necessary to a true understanding of the Christ impulse. It will be proved how absolute was its reality as a divine center of spiritual radiance, shining forth with a light that awakens an inner realization of that great truth reflected in these words of Goethe: There is a certain similarity between the relation of the colors and the light waves to the eye and the profound mystery of the inner Christ experience; as the eye apprehends the bright radiance of the light, so in human beings' deepest being do they become conscious of the divine essence—the Christ. That their souls can rise up and of their own effort transcend all previous limitations is now possible because the resplendent sun—that grand Mystery of Golgotha—has shed its glorious rays upon the world's history. If it were not for that supreme objective event and the objective Christ, there could be no such mysterious subjective inner experience as will enter into the life of humanity during the twentieth century, to be regarded earnestly and from a truly scientific standpoint.

Who overcomes himself, doth conquer that dread power
Which holds all beings closely bound—

One can say that only insofar as we connect ourselves to this
self-overcoming—to the Mystery of Golgotha, the Christ
Event—can we first discover the form that we have from our
earthly beginning, and see this as something from which we
must be redeemed and recognize that all moral activity and
cognition can only be approached through this redemption. It
will be through an understanding of inner salvation that
humanity will at last learn the true meaning of the concept of
redemption as related to life's historic evolution.

Finally, we would say that during the twentieth century there
will spread abroad a great illumination that will bring to
humanity a clear comprehension of the Christ impulse, and
this new knowledge will be in complete accord with the significance of Goethe's fuller message:

Who overcomes himself, doth conquer that dread power
Which holds all beings closely bound—and he shall rise.
First dawns the glorious truth in that glad hour;
That truth by which, through Christ, mankind shall gain
    God's prize.[23]

---

23. Von der Gewalt, die alle Wesen bindet,
    Befreit der Mensch sich, der sich überwindet,
    Und in dieser Überwindung sich selber erst in Wahrheit findet,
    Wie die ganze Menschheit in Christus sich selber in Wahrheit
    finden kann.

Printed in the United States
152815LV00001B/10/A